The Abingdon Women's Preaching Annual

Series 3
Year B

Compiled and Edited by

Beverly A. Zink-Sawyer

Abingdon Press
Nashville

THE ABINGDON WOMEN'S PREACHING ANNUAL

Copyright © 2002 by Abingdon Press

This book is printed on recycled, acid-free, elemental-chlorine–free paper.

ISBN 0-687-09584-0
ISSN 1086-8240

Scripture quotations, unless otherwise indicated, are from the *New Revised Standard Version of the Bible,* copyright 1989, the Division of Christian Education of the National Council of the Churches of Christ in the United States of America. Used by permission. All rights reserved.

Scripture quotations marked NIV are taken from the HOLY BIBLE, NEW INTERNATIONAL VERSION®. NIV®. Copyright © 1973, 1978, 1984 by International Bible Society. Used by permission of Zondervan Publishing House. All rights reserved.

Scripture quotations noted KJV are from the King James Version of the Bible.

Scripture quotations noted RSV are from the *Revised Standard Version of the Bible,* copyright 1946, 1952, 1971 by the Division of Christian Education of the National Council of the Churches of Christ in the United States of America. Used by permission. All rights reserved.

02 03 04 05 06 07 08 09 10 11 — 10 9 8 7 6 5 4 3 2 1

MANUFACTURED IN THE UNITED STATES OF AMERICA

In Loving Memory of

Eleanor Katherine Gohrs Zink

Woman of Wisdom, Woman of the Word

Contents

Introduction

For the past year, I have had the privilege of "living with" three extraordinary women of the nineteenth century. Antoinette Brown Blackwell, Olympia Brown, and Anna Howard Shaw were three of the first women ordained to the ministry of Word and sacrament by Protestant denominations in nineteenth-century America. Their lives and work are the focus of a sabbatical project in which I am presently engaged. These three women are remarkable in many ways, not least being the determined way in which they pursued their God-given calls to ordained ministry at a time when the idea of women in ministry was, at best, controversial and, at worst, unthinkable.

By the mid–nineteenth century, however, women's participation in a number of ecclesiastical roles had become commonplace. Women prayed, taught, testified, and even preached in "promiscuous" (i.e., comprised of men and women) religious gatherings. They were trained as religious educators and missionaries and sent to serve communities across the United States and across the world. They founded hospitals, schools, and reform organizations, all with the goal of serving God by serving those whom society had abandoned. With so many doors of the church opening to the gifts and service of women, it was inevitable by the second half of the nineteenth century that the ultimate church door, the door to ordained pastoral ministry, would open to them as well.

Brown Blackwell, Brown, and Shaw are unique in being among the first women ordained in America, but they stand in a long line of women preachers who preceded and have followed them. Indeed, preaching women have a long, proud tradition in the Christian church. It is often noted that women were the first preachers commissioned by Jesus, sent to the disciples—indeed, the whole world—with the command to "go, tell" what they had seen and heard on Easter morning. From that day on, women have been bold in their proclamation of faith despite the obstacles often placed in their paths. They found a way, with the grace and presence of God, to preach the good news of Jesus Christ even when there appeared to be no way. They organized house churches and founded convents; they wrote theological treatises and liturgical music and spiritual autobiographies; they taught, evangelized, and cared for people in all conditions and places. Most of all, these faithful female servants of God bore witness that the good news cannot be silenced; its messengers cannot be stilled. The Word of God always finds a way to be heard thanks to the Spirit and the spirit: the Spirit of God whose Word and work cannot be thwarted, and the indomitable spirit of women of faith who witness to the power of God's good news.

With this first volume in the third series of the *Abingdon Women's Preaching Annual*, we continue to celebrate the proud tradition of preaching women who proclaim the gospel and serve the church. In the pages that follow, I am delighted to share with the larger church the gifts of wonderful women preachers I have come to know in my own communities of faith and scholarship here in Virginia, across the country, and even across the world. Among them are women who represent twentieth-century "firsts" for women in the church, including the first woman ordained in Ireland, several women who were the first women to serve as pastors of particular congregations, and others who were among the first women to serve as senior pastors of churches in their denominations. Like the nineteenth-century clergywomen I am studying, these contemporary women do not regard themselves as unique in any way. They are simply being faithful to God's call to them, and good stewards of the gifts for ministry that God has given them.

Today is the day that the church has set aside to remember the martyrdom of some of the earliest women preachers. Perpetua, a young mother and woman of noble birth, her maid

Felicitas, and three of their companions were put to death in Carthage on the seventh of March, 203, for defying a Roman order to cease from proclaiming the Christian faith. Their words and witness remain many centuries later as testimony to the power of the gospel to endure ridicule, obstacles, and even death, for the Word of God always finds a way to be heard even when there appears to be no way. And so all of us who proclaim the gospel today—women and men alike—must stand in gratitude and awe of those like Perpetua and Felicitas, Antoinette, Olympia, and Anna, and all the faithful servants who have gone before us and followed the call of God.

Beverly A. Zink-Sawyer
March 7, 2001
Feast of Saints Perpetua and Felicitas
Richmond, Virginia

First Sunday of Advent

Ruth Patterson

Isaiah 64:1-9: The people of Israel acknowledge the greatness of God and their own sinfulness.

Psalm 80:1-7, 17-19: Rehearsing God's faithfulness in the past, the people plead for restoration and salvation by God.

1 Corinthians 1:3-9: Paul gives thanks to God for the steadfastness of the Christian believers at Corinth.

Mark 13:24-37: The devastations that will accompany the coming of the Son of Man are foretold with the warning to "keep awake."

REFLECTIONS

Reading Mark 13, it would seem to contain two main scenarios as Jesus foretells the future. The first appears to be a reference to the destruction of Jerusalem that took place some years after his death, and the second a reference to the Second Coming. It is possible, on a first perusal of these words, that we could be consumed with a sense of foreboding and fear as we go through a litany of predictions and dire warnings. To my mind, on further reflection, they convey a deep sense of confidence that, in spite of how things may seem at times, God is in control and holds all things in God's hands. That being so, we are encouraged to live as Advent people, as people of hope, who eagerly await the return of Christ. We are to be alert to the signs of the times, but not to be so sidetracked in trying to determine the day or the hour—as so many have been doing in the move from one millennium to another—that we fail to do the work assigned to us. The important thing is to so live life to the full, through him, with him, in him in the present, that when he does return, he will find us ready.

A SERMON BRIEF

Did you ever have the feeling that you could hardly wait until something happened, that if it didn't materialize soon you would just burst? I remember once, when I was a child, my father was away from home on what seemed to me to be an incredibly long trip. As the time drew near for his return, with the usual impatience of childhood I could hardly bear the waiting time. There were many conflicting emotions: excitement at the thought of seeing him, a great sense of love for the one who was not only father but friend, apprehension that something might happen that could delay his return, and yet, underlying everything else, the unquestioning trust of a child who knew that her father would be just as delighted to see her as she was to see him. And somehow, as we waited his coming, life had to be lived, normal duties performed, as well as the special preparations to welcome the beloved, for maybe, just maybe, he might come earlier than we expected, and it would never do if all was not in readiness for him when he came.

As part of the cycle of the Christian year, we come again to the very special time of Advent, the word that literally means "coming," when we "remember" (put flesh again onto) the God who came to us in Jesus, when we celebrate his presence with us now, and when we look forward to the time when he will come again to bring all things to their fulfillment. Advent is essentially a waiting time, an "in-between" time, a period between two very definite events—one that has happened and one that is promised but has still to materialize. How do we, as the church, as followers and friends of Jesus, wait in this time? When you've been waiting for something for a long while, it can be difficult to continue living with expectancy. When hope begins to fade, the vision becomes blurred. When hard trials come, when we personally enter the place of dereliction, or when sometimes the whole earth seems to be covered in darkness, the sense of advent can be anesthetized and the "in-between" becomes a no-man's-land where we drift aimlessly, or fall asleep because we cannot cope. We may pray, as did the prophet of old, "Oh that you would burst from the heavens and come down—and sort everything out," but our belief that this will actually ever happen, let alone that Christ might come earlier than expected, tends to be minimal or nonexistent.

I cannot help myself, but each year I approach the season of Advent with a sense of awe and wonder, as if my whole being is on tiptoe. For me it is a threshold time, a thin time, as if the veil between what we see and touch and know and the unseen world of mystery, of spiritual reality, is very fine and at any moment could be lifted. I have the sense of being surrounded by countless others from every age who are passionately waiting for the God who comes. We don't know when that will be. Not even the angels in heaven or Jesus himself know that; only God knows. And in a sense, it doesn't really matter. What does matter is what we do in the in-between time, in this threshold time; what matters is how we live right now. Do we wait passively or passionately? And if we're waiting passionately, then we're going to stay alert and keep watch, ready to pick up any sign of what God is doing, and to join in, to cooperate with God. If we have a passion for God, then that passion must translate itself into a resulting compassion for others, a yearning and an aching to see a world where justice and right relationships prevail, and a willingness to become makers rather than simply lovers of peace.

You know, there is a sense in which for us as Christians—as those who seek, however stumblingly, to be image bearers of Jesus—every day is Advent; every day is a *kairos* time. We are, could we but see, on the threshold of so much. God is pointing to countless doors of opportunity that God is opening for the bearers of good news, for those who will light a candle rather than curse the darkness. Not only that, God has equipped us, as Paul reminds us, with every spiritual gift we need as we eagerly await the return of Jesus. So there are no excuses for deserting the posts assigned to us, or for falling asleep, or for giving up any hope of Christ's return.

In terms of the story Jesus told, the role of the gatekeeper, the one who continually watches, is crucial. Where are the gatekeepers in the church today? I believe that they are the ones who watch in prayer, who refuse to give up but who keep on keeping on in faithful persistent prayer as they watch for his return. It is their prayer that enables the rest of us—if we have eyes to see and ears to hear—to truly be an Advent people; to perform the tasks assigned to us, as well as making special preparations to welcome the Beloved, for maybe, just maybe, he may come earlier than we expect, and it would never do if all were not in readiness for him when he comes.

SUGGESTIONS FOR WORSHIP

Call to Worship (from Psalm 80)

LEADER: Give ear, O Shepherd of Israel, you who lead Joseph like a flock!

15

PEOPLE:	**Stir up your might, and come to save us!**
LEADER:	Give us life, and we will call on your name.
PEOPLE:	**Restore us, O LORD of hosts; let your face shine, that we may be saved.**

Litany of Confession (from Isaiah 64)

LEADER:	We have all become like one who is unclean,
PEOPLE:	**And all our righteous deeds are like a filthy cloth.**
LEADER:	We all fade like a leaf,
PEOPLE:	**And our iniquities, like the wind, take us away.**
LEADER:	Yet, O LORD, you are our Father;
PEOPLE:	**We are the clay, and you are our potter; we are all the work of your hand.**
LEADER:	Do not be exceedingly angry, O LORD,
PEOPLE:	**And do not remember iniquity forever.**

Benediction (adapted from Mark 13)

And now go out into the world in peace. Beware, keep alert, for you do not know the hour when we will see the Son of Man coming in clouds with great power and glory. Be faithful in service and persistent in prayer; be Advent people, loving and serving the Lord. Amen.

Second Sunday of Advent

Elaine G. Siemsen

Isaiah 40:1-11: The prophet should encourage the people that God is here and that God cares for the nation as a shepherd cares for the flock.

Psalm 85:1-2, 8-13: God is the unity of love and loyalty, goodness and peace, and the result is justice.

2 Peter 3:8-15a: God desires for all to turn from sin and for no one to be lost. We have a responsibility to see to it that God finds us to be spotless and living in peace when God returns.

Mark 1:1-8: The content of the story is the good news about Jesus who is the Christ. This content contains the message that the time of God is at hand and we should prepare the path for the Lord to follow.

REFLECTIONS

These texts introduce the theme for the year. The second Sunday of Advent sends the preacher to the beginning of the story of God and God's people. Now the hearer knows that God's message and messenger of the good news have entered into history.

The beginning of the story is found in the first verse of Mark's text. Today's message is the good news about Jesus Christ, the Son of God. I have often interpreted these words to mean that the entire book of Mark is a Gospel, a genre of writing, and that it has as its subject Jesus Christ, who is the Son of God. Another interpretation of these verses tells us that Mark's words of introduction are describing the content of all that follows verse 1. Mark desires the reader/listener to know that in all the words that follow, the content of the good news is encapsulated.

If the preacher looks for the content of the good news in these opening verses, one encounters three separate locations that Mark illuminates. The good news can be found in the words of God's chosen prophets. In the prophetic content, the good news is the presence of God within all of creation. The second location is the actions of John the Baptizer. The content of the good news is the action of John through the ritual of washing for the forgiveness of sins, and within John's words about the one who is to come. The third and ultimate location of the content is the life, death, and resurrection of Jesus.

A SERMON BRIEF

A common game at Christmastime for my family was to guess the content of the presents either by shaking the boxes or by examining the packaging. We learned quickly that either method could deceive the person who received the gift. First, we discovered that special gift boxes were saved from one year to the next so the exterior was a deliberate attempt to mislead. Then we learned that there were many ways to disguise the contents. Extra packaging, multiple boxes, and added weight could all deceive the one opening the package.

Like Christmas packages, the content of our lives is often defined by what can be seen on the outside. Society tells us that pretty on the outside is more important than quality on the inside. Fashion and cosmetics companies encourage us to be deceptive about what is on the inside. We hide behind the appearance of the outer package of our lives.

Being deceptive about what is inside our lives, keeping who we are under the cover, is safe. When we let our real selves surface, we risk ridicule or rejection. Even within the church, there is an expectation of conformity. The woman who has had an abortion, the recovering Alcoholics Anonymous member, the child who lives in an abusive home know the need to maintain the pretty packaging while never exposing the true content of their lives. If the inside content is not as pretty as the outside packaging, others will gossip. The individual learns from the comments that they do not fit the acceptable mold.

Even happily married, "normal" children or productive older adults are encouraged to keep their true selves, the content of their lives, hidden. Others tell them that their faith, their love, their compassion are boring and outdated in this "postmodern," "post-Christian" world. Loving others or helping others is a messy business. The caring person will find that a life taken up with the concerns of others does not have the time or the inclination for beautifying the exterior as society demands. Dollars spent on cosmetic surgery can purchase months or even years of food for the hungry. Energy expended on creating a protected and beautiful package can help fill the empty lives of folk at the homeless shelter or the local nursing home. Manicured nails will be sacrificed, as hands spend time nurturing flowers to brighten the day of another.

Mark's introduction to this Advent season calls each of us to hear that the content of the good news is the life of Jesus. It is this content—*not* the packaging—that will restore in all of creation the love that God offers. There are in this story descriptions of many who will worry about external appearances. In spite of their efforts, deception or pretty packaging is not the first word, nor will it be the final word. It is the content of this package of good news that is clear for all who will listen.

Mark begins with the definitive statement that the content of the good news is Jesus the Christ, the one sent by God to restore all of creation to life with God. If the reader is at all unsure as to the identity of Jesus, it is the content of his life, death, and resurrection that should answer all questions. The reader is not to look exclusively at the pretty pictures of infancy narratives or the painful images of crucifixion. The reader is to look inside the person of Jesus to understand the content of the good news. Mark calls us to see the content of the good news in three different ways: through the tradition, time and history, and eternity.

The first facet of the contents of this package is that the good news is God's messenger. This is not another false prophet who will try to deceive the hearer through trickery or deception. Jesus is the one whom prophets foretold many generations before.

The second facet is that God's messenger is coming into our time and into our human history. This is not a story about a far-off galaxy. It is the story of the content of life in our time, in our human history. Lives have been and are being changed right now because of Jesus Christ who is the content of this message.

Finally, the third facet of the content of Mark's Gospel is that Jesus is the culmination of all of the content of God's love, will, and mercy intended for all creation. This content is a gift to all of creation, not just to the pretty, the few, the obvious.

We are challenged by the gospel, the content of the good news, to look at the life, death, and resurrection of Jesus. We then must use that new vision to find the echoes of that good news within our own lives. It all begins within this season of Advent. The challenge is to see past the pretty packaging of the culture, to see the true meaning of love and compassion that is the good news brought into each life through Jesus the Christ.

SUGGESTIONS FOR WORSHIP

Call to Worship

LEADER: Creator God, we gather this day to listen to your Word;

PEOPLE: Open our ears and hearts to hear your promise.

LEADER: We gather this day to make the good news the content of our lives;

PEOPLE: Encourage us to fill our lives with the life, death, and resurrection of Jesus the Christ.

LEADER: We seek the courage to change the inside of our lives so that we no longer seek just a pretty package for the world to see.

PEOPLE: Show us your love, O God, and love us into a new way of living.

Prayer of Confession

LEADER: Let us confess our sin before God and in the presence of one another.

ALL: Gracious God, you have given us the content for our lives. You have shared with us the life and love of Jesus the Christ. This day, we admit that we are more often worried about outward appearances before inner content. We look like Christians to impress our family and friends, but forget to live out the life of Christ. Fill us with your Word, make Jesus the content of all of our lives. Show us how to live out the good news in all that we say and do.

Assurance of Pardon

LEADER: Brothers and Sisters, God hears the cries of God's children. God forgives us for our weaknesses. God claims us anew this day, inviting each of us to "be filled with the Word and to live that Word in all the world." Amen.

Third Sunday of Advent

Vicki G. Lumpkin

Isaiah 61:1-4, 8-11: Isaiah proclaims the good news of "the year of the Lord's favor."

Psalm 126: A psalm of hope for restoration, for weeping turned to sowing, and tears turned to joy.

1 Thessalonians 5:16-24: Paul exhorts believers to rejoice, pray, and give thanks in all circumstances.

John 1:6-8, 19-28: A man named John is sent from God "to testify to the light."

REFLECTIONS

The texts for the third Sunday of Advent sound notes of joyful expectation. Pervading the lections are themes of mercy, deliverance, justice, restoration, and gratitude for God's gracious intervention in human affairs.

The Gospel reading for the day continues the account of the Baptizer, this time from the vantage point of the Fourth Gospel. John points to Christ while minimizing his own importance: "I am the voice of one crying out in the wilderness. Make straight the way of the Lord." Taking the role of witness, John points us to the unknown One who stands among us as the Light of the world. With his testimony, the wilderness of our existence becomes a venue of hope and liberation, a place where the Divine may be encountered and where illumination and transformation are holy possibilities.

As we follow in John's footsteps and testify to the Light, several questions arise: What is the message of hope and deliverance that we are called to cry out? How can we elicit an awareness that this place where we live, this wild place of grief and joy, of tragedy and celebration, is the very place where God's love and grace break into our daily lives? What do we need to make straight to allow the Lord unimpeded movement in our lives and hearts? As the people of God, God's ministers, what do we need to make straight to foster the Lord's unimpeded movement in the lives and hearts of those around us?

John's prophetic words remind all who truly seek that the One who came among us is also the One who will return, indeed, who already stands among us.

A SERMON BRIEF

Something's Coming

In the musical *West Side Story,* Tony, the lead male character, is reluctantly persuaded by his friends to come back to a world he had left, to the Jets, a New York City street gang. Although hesitant at first, his enthusiasm for the venture builds. In the excitement of being among old friends and in anticipation of new adventures that lie ahead, he sings a song entitled "Something's Coming."

As we move deeper into the experience of Advent, the Scripture readings call us to enter into a posture of joyful anticipation. Like the character in the musical, our excitement is building, but unlike him, we are not asked to return to the familiar world of our past, but to enter into a new place, a place of hope and expectation. "Something's coming," Advent tells us; it's time to get ready.

All four Gospel writers mention John the Baptist, but in the Fourth Gospel the evangelist is explicit in telling us that John's role was simply to witness, to tell the "truth, the whole truth, and nothing but the truth, so help him God" about Jesus. John the Baptist, the evangelist tells us, had a firm grasp of who he was and who he was not. John was a great man of God, but he was not God's love note to humankind, enfleshed in human form. John had a simple task—to help people get ready for the reality of God's salvation.

John was the "voice crying in the wilderness." The wilderness is an evocative image in the Scriptures. It is the "wild place" where the children of Israel learned what it meant to be the people of God. For forty years, the remaining life span of the Egypt-born generation, the children of Israel learned what it meant to listen, to follow, and to depend on the Lord. Their identity as the people of God was forged in the challenges and struggles of the wilderness. To hear the prophetic call of John involved both a literal and a figurative return to the wilderness, to the place of spiritual formation, to a place of divine encounter, to holy ground.

John's message was a simple one, so simple that the religious establishment had to send an official delegation to make sure they had heard it right. John simply said that God's salvation had come. "Who knows?" Tony sings in the musical, "I got a feeling there's a miracle due."

The Baptizer agrees. The miracle *is* due; in fact, John says, it is already here among us. The Light of the world stands in our midst. Following John's lead, we know two things: the miracle is not us, but with a wilderness perspective, we can point to Whom it is. We too are witnesses to this wonder.

What a miracle it is! The One for whom we wait already stands among us in the person of Jesus. In taking a human body, once again he has blessed our humanity and given tangible form to God's reconciling love. In the words of Isaiah 61:9, we are truly the people whom the Lord has blessed. We are blessed by God's presence, by God's intervention in our lives, by God's grace and love lavished upon us, poured out on people who often fail to recognize it.

For John tells us that the One for whom we wait stands unrecognized in our midst. He often appears in unexpected places and acts in surprising, unexpected ways. If we're not careful, we run the risk of overlooking him. We need to improve our vision, our recognition quotient. The question becomes, What are the things that prevent us from recognizing this miracle? Do we need to slow down? Do we need to remember to look for it? Do we need to take on an attitude of joy and anticipation? What are the things that need to be "made straight"—straightened out—in our lives? The Epistle reading for today gives us clues. We are called to live in a state of intimacy and communion with God, to do that which is good and avoid what is evil. That which keeps us from doing such things is to be removed so our access to God may be unhindered.

We may have some straightening out to do, but there is genuine good news! Whatever else we need to do, we need to recognize that the wilderness of our lives, that place marked by human celebration and mourning, challenge and testing, is also a place of holy encounter—holy ground. The "wild place" we inhabit on a daily basis is a habitation of the Extraordinary. We have not been abandoned. We don't have to wait until some future date to experience the miracle of God's grace.

Tony continues to sing: "And something great is coming!" Stephen Sondheim's lyrics from *West Side Story* capture the Advent spirit. Indeed, something wonderful, something beyond our wildest expectation is coming. It is right around the corner. God has spoken a Word of love, made it tangible, and set it in our midst. It is an incarnate, an enfleshed word of justice, mercy, and restoration.

"Who knows?" Tony sings, "Maybe tonight. . . ." The message of the Baptist is "maybe today!" And that is a message worth returning to the wilderness to hear; that is a message worth proclaiming. Let us rejoice and give thanks!

SUGGESTIONS FOR WORSHIP

Call to Worship (based on Isaiah 61:8-11)

LEADER: Let us rejoice in the Lord!
ALL: **Let us relish God's presence wholeheartedly!**
LEADER: For God has adorned us with salvation's finery,
ALL: **and bedecked us in garments of righteousness.**
LEADER: We are the people whom God has blessed.
ALL: **God's mercy will cause praise to spring up like flowers;**
LEADER: God's justice will produce a crop of righteousness.
ALL: **Let us rejoice in the Lord!**

Prayer of Confession (based on 1 Thessalonians 5:16-24)

Reconciling Lord, we confess that we often are not people of prayer. We fail to seek opportunities to give thanks in the varied circumstances of our lives. We do not cling to that which is good or refrain from that which is evil. We need your sanctifying mercy. Cleanse us and ready our hearts for a deeper experience of your indwelling presence. We ask these things in the name of the One who stands among us. Amen.

Assurance of Pardon

LEADER: Our assurance of pardon is found in the words of the apostle Paul: "The one who calls you is faithful, and God will do this."
ALL: **Thanks be to God, through Christ we are forgiven.**

Benediction

Depart with an Advent hope:
Messiah is coming, Christ is with us!
May the Lord of light
illumine your way,
chase away your darkness, and
by his presence transform your wilderness
into a garden of peace, liberty, and joy.
Amen.

Fourth Sunday of Advent

Gail Anderson Ricciuti

---

2 Samuel 7:1-11, 16: God promises to make David's name great and his house everlasting.

Luke 1:47-55 *or* **Psalm 89:1-4, 19-26:** The Magnificat of Mary and the psalm it echoes.

Romans 16:25-27: A doxology of Paul praising the revelation of Jesus Christ to all.

Luke 1:26-38: The birth of Jesus is foretold to Mary by the angel Gabriel.

REFLECTIONS

Two evocative texts are brought together on this day, like agates in a rock tumbler, to polish against each other. One is Luke's amazing announcement that there will be a Son, that the frail tent of flesh and bone will be pervaded in a new way by divine Being and carried first in the temporary shelter of one young female body. In the other, from 2 Samuel 7, we overhear Yahweh's dialogue with David regarding what dwelling is appropriate for Israel's God.

This fourth and final Sunday of Advent rushes toward Incarnation; and its theological questions (How? Why? For what purpose?) always tread the edge of mystery. The Creator and Deliverer of Israel chooses to come cloaked in the frailest of membranes: human flesh. Writing later than Luke, John would express mystery and earthiness in the same breath, writing of Word becoming flesh and literally "pitching a tent" among us.

Young Mary is asked to become the first "tent" erected by the Word—the first temporary, temporal dwelling for the Incarnate One. Life is mysterious *enough* when you are only twelve or fourteen, as she may have been; childhood no longer fits. *Nothing* fits exactly right. You are arms and legs and feet, with a face part girl and part woman, and a body shape-shifting out of control, inhabited by longings that fill you with both ecstasy and fear. In that light, her bodily circumstances intensify the nuances of fragility and risk into which God chooses to enter. The metaphor of the tent—the sort of dwelling preferred by God—evokes a profusion of memories for anyone who has experienced what "tenting" entails. To let the metaphor tell us what incarnation means is to understand "God with us" in a new way.

A SERMON BRIEF

The God Who Camps Out

Are you the one to build me a house to live in? I have not lived in a house since the day I brought up the people of Israel from Egypt to this day, but I have been moving about in a tent and a tabernacle. (2 Samuel 7:5-6)

Christmas in the Northern Hemisphere is an odd time to think about camping, but the wonderful serendipity of the texts for today carries this communiqué: This God *likes* living in a tent.

Having experienced countless more than a hundred and one wilderness nights, I've had ample time to ponder what that might mean. In a tent beside a lost lake one night, you lie wakeful, knowing that you are miles from anyone who would notice if you didn't return. The night sweats take hold of you, as you fantasize that a sudden noise or flash of lightning startles a moose out in the bush, and that moose stampedes blindly into the clearing, trampling you—tent and all—in its frantic wake. Just then the forest rumbles and real hoofbeats gallop by.

Another summer night, the ground under you moans distantly, and nine months later the mountain explodes not two miles from where you'd laid your ear.

Yet another summer, beside another lake, you hear quiet snuffling three inches away, on the other side of the thin nylon wall.

And at 2 A.M. in mid-July somewhere near the Arctic Circle, you open your eyes because the back of your eyelids, and the tent itself, are alight with the sun. Constant reminders, all: in a tent, you have only a membrane for protection (which is no defense at all). The startling news of Advent is that this is what God prefers, even longs for—not to be walled away from the world, but to experience unprotected the nuances of weather and light and risk.

27

And so it is easy to understand why this God can't stand to have windows closed, cannot abide hermetically sealed spirits, chooses not to reside permanently among any tribes, even (or especially) those who think themselves divinely ordained. "Would you build me a house to live in?"

This freely moving One came into Mary's carefully planned, socially delineated life with an upheaval that she could never have expected. She was a girl properly engaged—all events in her young existence following their appropriate, prescribed trajectory—until this. And here was a God who would rather be with those who don't expect him.

What is it about Mary that makes her an appropriate object of God's grace? The text does not tell us; she is identified simply as a young girl engaged to be married. Luke reveals more about Zechariah and Elizabeth, describing them as living righteous and blameless lives. Mary, however, doesn't seem to earn or deserve the honor of a visitation more than anyone else. But recognizing this to be God's plan, not her own, she gives her consent: "Let it be with me according to your word."

As Samuel's narrative depicts it, when David resolves to perform a monumental act of piety and erect a mighty temple for Yahweh, his idea meets with divine demolition by the God who doesn't want or need a temple. This "free, mobile, dynamic God—sojourns, bivouacs, and comes and goes, but never settles and becomes confined in one place."[1]

David had hoped to build Yahweh a temple; but Yahweh turns the tables and promises to make David "a house"—a dynasty that finds its ultimate, unexpected fruition in the willingness of Mary's incarnational, Advent faith.

With all the forest sounds surrounding me that distant night, I lay in terror of my imagined moose stampede; but I would not for all the world give up hearing those ghostly beautiful hoofbeats race past me, out of darkness and away into darkness. The moment will stay with me for the rest of my life, along with a dream that followed: I was in the presence of a friend and teacher, in a log cabin somewhere, and we were laughing and singing to each other. Suddenly I stopped in midstanza and said, "I love you!" She put her arm across my shoulders—so tangibly that I woke up, convinced she had really been next to me. In that waking, I realized through and through that the night's earlier terror was gone. I was at home as a nomad, at home in this wilderness place. Was it "only a dream"?

The membrane of a tent, if we have courage to inhabit it, is too thin to protect us. But perhaps Christ enters human flesh as a way of putting his arm around our shoulders and making us at home in this frail tent that he honors, if we concur with the will that would make it his dwelling. May Jesus the Christ abide in our tents, now and all our days.

SUGGESTIONS FOR WORSHIP

Call to Worship (based on Psalm 89:1-4)

LEADER: Sing, people of God, sing of God's steadfast love forever!
PEOPLE: **With our mouth we will proclaim the Lord's faithfulness to all generations.**
LEADER: Declare that steadfast love is forever established.
PEOPLE: **God's faithfulness is as firm as the heavens.**
LEADER: For a covenant has been made with the chosen one, and God has sworn it.
ALL: **We will sing God's steadfast love forever!**

Prayer of Confession (based on Luke 1:45-55)

God of all promise, holy *is* your name. But we are forgetful of your mercy, consumed with personal struggles for status and survival. Forgive us, Mighty One, for disregarding you, the Source of our strength. Corral and quiet the proud strategies of our hearts, lest we be scattered far from your goodness. Fulfill our hungers with the nourishment of your spirit, lest in endless acquisition we find ourselves empty at last. We would offer our illusory powers into your hands, so that we might become your humble and thankful people once more, in Jesus' name.

Assurance of Pardon

LEADER: In remembrance of his mercy, God has helped servant Israel. In Jesus Christ, we are forgiven.
PEOPLE: **My soul magnifies the Lord!**
LEADER: And blessed is the one who believes there will be a fulfillment of what the Lord has promised.
PEOPLE: **My spirit rejoices in God my Savior!**

Benediction (based on Romans 16:25-27)

LEADER: May our wise and able God strengthen you,
through the precious mystery now revealed,
the prophetic message made known,
and the strong, compelling Spirit of faith.

PEOPLE: **Glory to God forever, through Jesus Christ, the
revelation of Love! Amen.**

1. Walter Brueggemann, in *Texts for Preaching: A Lectionary Commentary Based on the NRSV-Year B,* ed. Walter Brueggemann, et al. (Louisville: Westminster John Knox Press, 1993), 32.

Christmas Eve

Marjorie A. Menaul

Isaiah 9:2-7: Isaiah prophesies the coming of a righteous ruler.

Psalm 96: The psalmist sings praise to God who will come to "judge the world with righteousness."

Titus 2:11-14: Paul declares to Titus that the grace of God has appeared in the glory of Jesus Christ.

Luke 2:1-14 (15-20): The story of the birth of Jesus and the angelic announcement to the shepherds.

REFLECTIONS

On Christmas Eve, the church is full of people—young and old, friends and strangers. Especially in a tradition where the celebration of the Eucharist is the climax of worship, a Christmas Eve sermon needs to be relatively brief. The reflection presented here lies in the background of the sermon that follows, and on another occasion might have formed the first section of the sermon.

Whose baby was he?

He was Mary's child, certainly—when a baby is born, it's difficult to mistake the mother.

And who was the father? Was it Joseph, who accepted her child as his own (in Luke's Gospel, without any obvious struggle)? Was it God, who would claim him as "my Son" at his baptism? Yes and yes. A baby with two fathers—problematic from the start.

And as Luke tells it, Joseph was not the only man who had to wrestle with questions about exactly whose baby Jesus was. The shepherds were faced with a difficult question as well. Their line of work meant that they and their families were at the low end of society. A shepherd had to be away from home night after night, leaving his wife alone. Who knew what might happen to her or what she might do? Shepherding families had little honor, because nobody could be certain of the fatherhood of the children.

31

So when shepherds out on the hillsides were told "to you a baby has been born," the announcement must have raised questions, even red flags, in their minds. Who exactly had given birth? A wife? A daughter? And who had fathered the newborn child? Those of us who live two thousand years later may hear only hope and joy in the promise, "to you is born a Savior," but for those who first heard it, the words "to you is born" would surely have aroused both confusion and concern.

"My baby? I wasn't expecting a baby. What exactly has been going on while I wasn't looking? This child who has been born—how is he *my* child?"

The first answer to that question, of course, is that the shepherds were Israelites—not highly respected ones, but Israelites nevertheless. Their nation was subject to the rule of Rome, and while some Israelites chafed under foreign domination, others drew power from it. It was a dead-end situation, with no relief in sight. Until God acted.

For a child has been born for us, a son given to us.

The prophet Isaiah had written those words long before, to people enduring the threat of foreign domination in their own time. Although Isaiah had no thought of Jesus, we who live on the other side of the Incarnation can hear in them the promise that Israel would find its deliverance in Jesus Christ.

Whose child was Jesus? As the fulfillment of prophecy, Jesus was born the child of all Israel, but his coming was not for the salvation of Israel alone. Jesus was born the child of all humanity. Isaiah had anticipated this truth when he said, about Galilee of the nations, about *Gentiles*:

> The people who walked in darkness
>   have seen a great light;
> those who lived in a land of deep darkness—
>   on them light has shined.

Whose baby was he? As Luke sees it, Jesus was, and is, the child of God, of Mary and Joseph, of Israel, of outcasts, and of all humanity. Not just on the cross, but from the very beginning, God has been busy giving Jesus away to anyone who would receive him.

A SERMON BRIEF

The gifts we give at Christmas, and the ways in which we receive them, show a lot about who we are. Every family has its traditions, and it's important that the process of unwrapping be done in the proper way. Of course, what is "proper" varies from household to household.

For some of us, the unwrapping will begin right after church on Christmas Eve. For others, it will mean leaping out of bed as early as possible on Christmas Day, or rolling out of bed as late as possible—children and adults tend to pull in different directions on that one. It may mean everybody taking turns to open and discuss and admire; it may mean everybody ripping into a stack of presents and showing them off afterward. It's not just what's in the package that matters; how we get to it is important as well.

And tonight is the time when the expectation is highest. The time of preparation is over. We've listed and shopped and ordered and wrapped. Now—at last—it's almost time to start unwrapping.

I'm not just humoring the children here—Christmas is not a celebration particular to children. Fellow grown-ups, let's not be too adult about it. Every one of us needs to receive presents as well as to give them. We need signs of love, tokens that someone else knows and cares who we are and what we enjoy. In particular, every one of us needs to receive the present we celebrate tonight.

Jesus, the child of God, came into the lives of Mary and Joseph as a gift—a firstborn son, the continuation of their heritage and their families. He came to the shepherds as a gift: "To you is born this day in the city of David a Savior." He comes to us as a gift as well. The most important Christmas present of all is not something that waits for you at home under the tree, but the gift God has given to all of us together. Jesus is our Christmas present.

He's harder to unwrap than the presents tied up in paper and ribbon. We won't get Jesus all unwrapped tonight, or tomorrow, or in the next twelve days. As he lived on the earth—the child of Mary and Joseph and Israel—the gift of God-with-us kept getting unwrapped, layer after layer. It was unwrapped as Jesus grew and taught and healed and lived and died and rose. We continue to unwrap it as the church struggles with times that change, and human nature that stays the same.

In the gift of Jesus, the love of God (which is what we need the most) is given to us in different ways, according to our needs. When

33

he was born at Bethlehem, Jesus was like a box that hadn't been opened yet. The ribbon and the wrapping were pulled away as he taught and helped people and made them well. People thought he was a troublemaker, and they killed him for it—which is even sadder than when your best present gets broken on Christmas morning. But this present didn't stay broken. Because God, who is at work in the world to fix what is broken, raised Jesus from the dead. The world is broken, and so are we.

But "unto us is born a Savior." That's our Christmas present.
Tonight, and tomorrow,
through the twelve days of Christmas,
and all the years of your life—
keep unwrapping!

SUGGESTIONS FOR WORSHIP

Call to Worship (from Isaiah 9 and Luke 2)

The people who walked in darkness have seen a great light;
those who lived in a land of deep darkness—on them light has shined.
Glory to God in the highest heaven,
and on earth, peace among those whom God favors.

Prayer of Confession

LEADER: God sent God's Son into the world to shine the light of his truth into our hearts and to set us free from the darkness of despair. Let us confess our sin and open ourselves to God's gracious forgiveness in Jesus Christ. Let us pray:
Eternal God, Mary rejoiced in your call to bear the Christ Child. We do not always heed your call to us as joyfully. We reject your claim on our lives, following instead our selfish ways.

PEOPLE: **Forgive us and remake us, O Lord.**

LEADER: Jesus was born in humble circumstances and wandered the land to preach and teach. We insist on our own comforts while ignoring the poverty and needs of others. We pursue material riches at the expense of the impoverishment of our souls.

PEOPLE:	**Forgive and remake us, O Lord.**
LEADER:	Angels proclaimed the "good news of great joy" that had come into the world with the birth of the Christ Child. We are timid in sharing the good news of your truth with our world.
PEOPLE:	**Forgive us and remake us, O Lord.**
LEADER:	The shepherds watching their flocks on the hillside near Bethlehem followed with wonder to see the great thing God had done. We remain entrenched in familiar, comfortable places, failing to see the new things you are doing in our lives.
PEOPLE:	**Forgive us and remake us, O Lord, we pray. Amen.**

Benediction

May Christ, who in the Incarnation gathered into one things earthly and heavenly, fill us and all creation with joy and peace. Amen.[1]

1. Adapted from *The Book of Occasional Services* (New York: The Church Hymnal Corporation, 1979), 21.

Epiphany of the Lord

Donna Hopkins Britt

Isaiah 60:1-6: The light and hope of God are promised to the people of Zion who have long lived in despair.

Psalm 72:1-7, 10-14: The psalmist prays for a just and righteous ruler.

Ephesians 3:1-12: The apostle Paul confirms the place of Gentiles in the promise of Christ.

Matthew 2:1-12: Wise men from the East seek and find the Christ Child.

REFLECTIONS

Life is a constant search: a search for balance, for guidance, for understanding and wisdom. The older I get, the more comfortable I have become with mystery, with the fact that some questions will always remain unanswerable. In the Ephesians passage, Paul writes about the mystery of Christ, but then says that he is trying "to make everyone see [or "bring to light" as the *New Oxford Annotated Bible* suggests] what is the plan of the mystery hidden for ages in God who created all things" (3:9). Isaiah, too, talks about bringing things into the light. "Lift up your eyes and look around," he proclaims (60:4); come from the darkness to the light.

It was the light of the star that led the Magi to find Jesus. In a world of intangibles, still there are many tangible places to find Jesus. We have only to set our minds on *looking* for him—and taking the necessary steps of faith to find him.

A SERMON BRIEF

Where the Star Stops

It was the height of the Great Depression, the early 1930s, when plans for the Hoover Dam were being made. You might assume correctly that Herbert Hoover was president. Each spring, the flooding of the Colorado River challenged the farmers who tried to eke out their livelihood on the land near the river. It was decided that a massive dam was the solution. Long before construction could begin, however, the first big question to be answered was, *Where? Where,* along all the river's canyons and gorges, could this monstrous project be built? *Where* would it best block the torrents to control flooding, to initiate irrigation systems, and to operate the turbines for hydroelectric power? *Where* could a dam like this have the most benefits? After deciding the dam was needed, the first big question was, *Where?*

The "Where?" question also plays a significant part in the Gospel story of the Magi. Certain sky configurations or bright stars were said to signify the birth of a royal baby, so these Magi, or astrologers or wise men, followed a star from the East in search of this royal child.

The first stop for the wise men was Jerusalem. We assume there were three, because we learn later that they bore three gifts. It seems that the star had led them there first, and they came with the question, *Where?* "Where is the child who has been born king of the Jews?" they asked. "For we have observed his star at its rising, and have come to pay him homage." *Where* is the child?

The Magi were on a journey of faith. For some people, a journey of faith would be driving to the Super Bowl with one hundred dollars and no tickets. These guys went further and deeper. Imagine leaving your home to follow a *star*. You don't know how long you'll be gone; you don't know whose land you will be crossing or how many weapons the owners have; you don't know how rough the terrain will be; and you especially don't know where you'll end up.

Nothing is said about the dangers the Magi faced along their route, or how they had the courage even to begin their trip. What we do know is that the first leg of their journey of faith took them to Jerusalem. And although Jerusalem was the "faith capital" of Judaism, the child-king was not to be found there. In fact, King Herod helped the Magi by learning and then telling them that the prophet Micah had foretold that a ruler—one who could challenge Herod's authority—would be born in Bethlehem, just six miles away.

Herod was frightened by what he learned, so he conspired to send the Magi *to* Bethlehem, commanding them to bring word when they found this king, so Herod, too, could pay him homage. Herod appears a bit like the Grinch here, rubbing his paws together and plotting how he would rid himself not of Christmas, as did the Grinch, but of the Christ. So the Magi continued their journey of faith, following the star south to Bethlehem until the star—their guide—told them where to stop. Scripture tells us the reaction of the Magi: "When they saw that the star had stopped, they were *overwhelmed with joy.*" That was *before* they checked inside to see if it was the right place!

Of course, it was. Inside, they found Mary and the child, and knelt before Jesus to pay him homage, opening their treasure chests to present him with gifts of gold and expensive fragrances befitting his royalty.

The Magi searched for Jesus and were rewarded when they found him. Whenever *we* seek Jesus, we also will be rewarded with joy when we find him. If we seek him in our jobs and chores, we will find him in our jobs and chores. If we seek Jesus at church, we will find him at church. If we seek Jesus in the person who is driving us crazy, we will find him in that person. Wherever we seek and find Jesus, like the Magi, we will be overwhelmed with joy.

Along with the joy of finding Jesus, we also discover a mysterious pull to want to follow Jesus. Even then, the question *Where?* remains with us as it did with those who first followed the star: *Where* will he lead us? *Where* will we stop along the way? *Where* will we be able to rest? Will the terrain be difficult? What obstacles will we encounter along the way?

Most of us don't like to live with unanswered questions, to live with the mystery. But the life of faith requires it. We trust that God will answer the questions when we need the answers and will guide our steps in the meantime. Each year the church celebrates Epiphany on January 6, the day after the twelfth day of Christmas. On Epiphany, we celebrate the Magi finding Jesus: God made visible to non-Jews. And although the unique star of Bethlehem has long since faded from the sky, in its place of leadership now is the one *to whom it led* more than two thousand years ago. Jesus Christ is now the one to follow. And just as following the star was a journey of faith for the Magi, following Jesus is a journey of faith for us.

Legend has it that Confucius said: "A journey of a thousand miles begins with a single step." This is true in a physical journey as well as in the journey of faith. One step of faith will lead to another, more important step of faith. And since we are all at different places, that step will be different for each person. As a new year begins, your new year's resolutions could take the form of steps of faith. Your step could be to join your heart and spirit and energy with a congregation of believers, or to deepen your involvement in the church. A step of faith could be encouraging a family member or friend on his or her spiritual journey. A step of faith could be reading the Bible every day, or starting a Bible study group. A step of faith could be reaching out in loving service to others.

The Magi invite us to put on our walking shoes, pray for God's guidance as to where our first steps should be, and then move forward with confidence into the new year, into a new or renewed relationship with God. You've made one step of faith by being here this morning. *Where* will your next step take you?

SUGGESTIONS FOR WORSHIP

Call to Worship (based on Isaiah 60)

LEADER: Arise, shine; for your light has come,
PEOPLE: And the glory of the Lord has risen upon you.
LEADER: Lift up your eyes and look around,
PEOPLE: Then you shall see and be radiant; your heart shall thrill and rejoice.
LEADER: We are called to be attentive to God's light and love.
PEOPLE: Let us soak up God's light to reflect it to the world.

Prayer of Confession

Loving God, too often we live in the dark. We feel around with our hands until we find what we think we need, but somehow we avoid searching for the light switch that you hold. Forgive us for trying to live as if we have all the necessary resources. Help us open our eyes to see the light that shines around you, so that we may become radiant, too. You are all we need. Help us find you as we seek and find Jesus the Christ. In his name we pray. Amen.

Assurance of Pardon

Jesus is the light of the world, and in turning toward him, we find him. In asking forgiveness, he gives it with grace and generosity. Friends, believe the good news of the gospel; in Jesus Christ we are forgiven.

Benediction

May you go from this place with blessed and renewed spirits, attentive to the presence of God, and reflecting God's light to the world.

Baptism of the Lord

Elizabeth Bridges Ford

Genesis 1:1-5: God creates the heavens and the earth, light and darkness, day and night.

Psalm 29: The psalmist praises the God of all creation.

Acts 19:1-7: Paul baptizes believers in Ephesus in the name of the Lord Jesus, and they receive the Holy Spirit.

Mark 1:4-11: Jesus is baptized by John and confirmed in his mission by God's voice from heaven.

REFLECTIONS

Friends of mine had the privilege of witnessing an Orthodox baptism in Syria. They watched as a naked baby was plunged repeatedly into a baptismal font, his screams sounding throughout the sanctuary.

The violence of the scene mirrors the language in Mark's account of Jesus' baptism. Matthew and Luke report that the heavens "opened" as Jesus was coming up out of the water, but in Mark, the heavens are being "torn apart." The Greek word *schizo* captures the drama of the moment. The curtain of heaven is ripped open, and the seam cannot be mended.

Few of us experience anything so dramatic at our baptisms. The voice from heaven and the Spirit's descent are neither audible nor apparent. Yet baptism is a significant event in the life of faith. It marks our public entrance into Christian community, just as it signals the advent of Jesus' public ministry.

Some parents liken baptism to the first day of kindergarten, a day that is equally as momentous for parents as for children. For children, the first day of school is a rite of passage. For parents, it is the beginning of letting go.

Perhaps this is why the voice from heaven sounds so clearly. "You are my Son, the Beloved; with you I am well pleased." Isn't this the knowledge that we hope all parents will want to instill in their children, that they are loved for who they are? As our children venture into the world, we long for them to carry with them this inner certainty.

We long for this, yet so often our hopes are thwarted. Hurtful words, pressure to belong, feelings of uncertainty and inadequacy may lodge themselves in any of us, leading us to stray from our true selves and from the knowledge that God loves us.

Baptism reminds us of who we are and calls us to surround others with God's love, so that they, too, may reclaim their identity as God's beloved children.

A SERMON BRIEF

My five-year-old cousin Abby circled the table after dinner. When she came to her dad, she crawled up in his lap. The conversation continued around them while Abby and her dad shared a private moment. Unaware of anyone else in the room, he told her quietly, "I am so blessed that you are my daughter. You are a beautiful girl. You make me so happy." It was a tender moment, a holy moment between a parent and child.

Mark's story of Jesus' baptism gives us a glimpse into another holy moment. It is so holy that God can't be contained a moment longer. As Jesus is coming up out of the waters of the Jordan, he sees the heavens being torn apart and the Spirit descending into him like a dove. A voice from heaven says, "You are my Son, the Beloved; with you I am well pleased." There is no hint that anyone else sees or hears anything, but Jesus hears, "You are my Son, the Beloved; with you I am well pleased."

One scholar says that at this moment, the barrier between heaven and earth was ripped apart. Just as the temple curtain is "torn in two from top to bottom" at Jesus' death, the heavens are torn apart at his baptism (15:38). Now humanity has full access to God, and God is "on the loose in our realm."[1] The rupture is permanent. Nothing will be the same again.

This is the beginning of Mark's story of Jesus. God, who can't be silent a moment longer, speaks. This is the same God who spoke creation into being, the same God who told Moses, "I AM WHO I AM," the same God who cried out through the prophets. God speaks.

"You are my Son, the Beloved; with you I am well pleased." Do you hear the echoes of the Hebrew Scriptures? The words "You are my Son" appear in the Psalms (Ps. 2:7), "with you I am well pleased," and in Isaiah (Isa. 42:1). And the beloved Son recalls another beloved son—Isaac, son of Abraham (Gen. 22:2). "You are my Son, the Beloved; with you I am well pleased."

Matthew begins with Jesus' genealogy, Luke with Jesus' birth. Only Mark begins with his baptism. It is significant that Mark places this scene at the very beginning of Jesus' ministry, before he has done anything. The voice from heaven affirms that Jesus is God's beloved child, the one with whom God is "well pleased." This is who Jesus is, apart from anything he does or doesn't do.

It is an important message for us to hear as well, for Jesus' story mirrors our story. In baptism, we, too, find our identity. We learn who we are in God's eyes. Baptism signifies many things: washing, cleansing, new birth, incorporation into the community of faith. Baptism also seals a person's identity as a beloved child of God. *This* is who we are.

Sometimes feelings of anger, inadequacy, failure, or guilt obscure the persons we truly are. We expend so much energy constructing what Thomas Merton calls a "false self"—the self we project, the person that others think we are, the self we create to protect ourselves—but this self isn't always consonant with who we are in God's eyes. This "false self" is an illusion, a mask of our own making.[2] Hidden behind the masks we wear is our "true self," the one created in God's image, the one who is beloved of God.[3]

In this season of resolutions and fresh starts, baptism reminds us of a new beginning that is open to each one of us. We can wade into the waters of renewal, remembering our baptism. Cleansed of our false selves, we begin a lifelong process of learning to live as God's beloved. We grow to know for ourselves that God loves us for who we are.

Imagine how different our lives would be if we truly believed that the creator of the universe loves us for who we are. We would live out of faith, not out of fear.

As a community of faith, we are called to nurture others, to help them grow into their identity as God's beloved children. Jesus' own ministry is shaped by this knowledge, and so is ours. As we open ourselves to receive God's love, we free ourselves to share it.

A colleague tells the story of a missionary who worked in the South Pacific. In the village where he lived there was a custom that when a woman was engaged, her husband-to-be would give her family a gift. To express his appreciation, he would give them a cow because cows were considered precious.

A family of high status might receive two cows when their daughter married. One family in the village received three cows because their daughter's husband was so grateful. But in this same family, there was an older sister who had never attracted the attention of the village suitors. She had given up hope of being married. You could see it in the way she walked, with her head down, her shoulders stooped, as if she were ashamed to be seen.

An islander came to the village and took notice of the woman. In time, he approached her parents and asked to marry her. He gave them his gift—a gift of ten cows. This was unheard of, to be a "ten cow" woman.

The couple left, and when the woman returned to the village several years later, no one recognized her. She stood tall and proud. She acted like a "ten cow" woman. She was transformed by love into the person she truly was.

In God's eyes, we are all "ten cow" men and women. Let us stand tall and proud and go into the world confident in God's love and grace, for God has spoken.

SUGGESTIONS FOR WORSHIP

Call to Worship

LEADER: Come, all you people.
PEOPLE: **Come from far and near.**
LEADER: Come to the fountain of forgiveness.
PEOPLE: **Come to the river of life.**
LEADER: Come, wade in the water and be refreshed.

Prayer of Confession

Holy God, Giver of Life, we confess that we are parched for your presence. We stand at the water's edge but refuse your gift of love. Speak to us, O God. Teach us to accept your love. Open our hearts to hear your voice. Help us listen to your Word of forgiveness and grace.

Assurance of Pardon (based on Psalm 29)

May the God of grace give you strength.
May the Lord of life bless you with peace.

Benediction

Go in peace, confident that you are a "ten cow" child of God.
May you hear the voice of heaven,
May you feel the Spirit's presence,
May you see the face of Christ in all whom you meet.

1. Donald Juel, *A Master of Surprise: Mark Interpreted* (Minneapolis: Fortress Press, 1994), 35.
2. Thomas Merton, *New Seeds of Contemplation* (New York: New Directions, 1961), 34-36.
3. Ibid., 31.

Transfiguration of the Lord

Felecia T. Douglass

2 Kings 2:1-12: Elisha inherits Elijah's mantle.

2 Corinthians 4:3-6: God's glory is revealed in Jesus.

Psalm 50:1-6: The psalmist praises God's power and might.

Mark 9:2-9: The transfiguration of Jesus.

REFLECTIONS

This broader section begins with the Petrine confession and Jesus' rebuke of Peter. Next, Jesus instructs his disciples to take up their cross and follow him. Then six days later, Jesus takes Peter, James, and John to the mountain where they will witness the transfiguration. The Divine often chooses a mountaintop like Sinai from which to speak. On this mountain, Moses and Elijah flank Jesus. Ironically, Jesus climbs another hill, Golgotha, this time flanked by two thieves.

God transfigures Jesus, and he shines with God's glory. Here God confirms Jesus' identity by repeating the words heard at his baptism. God also adds, "Listen to him!" Jesus was God's Son, and in following him, the disciples were on the right track.

This is a narrative sermon about a friend of mine named Sandy, who, like the disciples, was unsure that she was on the right track. Then, in one small way, the voice of God changed her despair and gave her the strength to continue.

This sermon was preached at the Vass Presbyterian Church in Vass, North Carolina. This is a small, faithful congregation whose members often wonder if they are valuable. In their struggling, I wanted them to see God's glory—glory that is always lurking beneath the surface. Glory that by the grace of God, they too share.

A SERMON BRIEF

On the Right Track

Sandy Ballard plowed through her day's errands, head down, eyes vacant. She was preoccupied. More than that, she was dejected, confused, and wondering what to do next. She was coaching her son's soccer team because there weren't enough dads to coach, and here they were, halfway through the season, and they hadn't won a single game; hadn't even come close.

She knew winning wasn't everything, but they were a great team and they should win some. It wasn't their fault. It was hers. She was no coach and she knew it. Sandy assumed that interest in coaching, willingness to coach, and good physical condition was all she needed.

Well, that, and a coaching seminar. She went to the seminar; learned the soccer drills; ate, drank, and slept the rule book; led the team in stretches and calisthenics; jogged laps around the field; devised strategies; and cheered them on until she was hoarse. None of it worked. Nothing she did worked. She must have forgotten something, but Sandy couldn't think of anything else to do.

There was one thing left to do; she could quit. Rick Williams was available to take her team. He went to her church and was an experienced soccer coach. He could take these talented kids and make them into a winning team. He could succeed where she had failed. Sandy resolved to call him after dinner that night.

She felt better once she had made the decision. She picked up the pace for her last errand, and turned onto Carthage Street. She was going to pick up a pair of shoes at the repair shop. She reached for the door handle, but stopped. Someone had called her name, "Coach Sandy! Hey, Coach Sandy!" She turned and saw Scott Patton hanging out the window of his mom's car. More than half of his body was sticking out that window, and a goofy smile was plastered on his face. He was waving his arms back and forth so she would see him, all the while hollering, "Coach Sandy! Coach Sandy!"

Sandy smiled and waved back, and in an instant, something happened to her. Something changed when she heard that six-year-old's voice. A transformation occurred, and she would never be the same again. At that very moment, on Carthage Street, outside the Nunnery Shoe Repair Shop in Sanford, North Carolina, Sandy Ballard became a soccer coach.

She was on the right track after all. There was no reason to quit.

She was doing it right, even though things hadn't quite worked out. The voice confirmed it. Sandy's confusion lifted, and her spirits soared. You could tell it by the way she walked, face bright, head held high. They might never win a game, but she was their soccer coach. She was on the right track.

Confused and despairing, needing to know if they were on the right track, Peter, James, and John went with Jesus to the mountain. Maybe he would take back the things he had just told them: how he would be arrested, stand trial, and eventually die. His words confused and frightened them.

They'd seen the miracles and heard the teachings. Peter spoke for them all when he'd confessed Jesus was the Christ, God's anointed. He also spoke for them when he'd corrected Jesus. A suffering Messiah was incomprehensible. At the very least, they thought Jesus owed them an explanation. They had given up everything to follow him. Were they on the right track?

While they climbed, Peter remembered other mountaintop experiences. God often picked a mountaintop to show God's glory and might. Maybe God would shed some light on their confusion.

When they reached the top of the mountain, something indescribable happened to Jesus. He was clothed in white. His face shone like the sun. He looked like a flash of lightning. Then Elijah and Moses appeared with Jesus, one on his right and one on his left. They stood with Jesus in that crackling circle of light. The wind blew and a cloud of light overshadowed them all.

Like a mighty chorus of angels, God's voice came out of the cloud, "This is my Son, the Beloved; listen to him!" The disciples were so overcome with fear, they fell face down on the ground. When they opened their eyes, they were alone.

As they climbed down the mountain, Jesus ordered them to tell no one what they had seen. Later, as they made their way to Jerusalem, Jesus told them two more times that he would be rejected, suffer, and die. Only a short time after this mountaintop experience, Jesus would climb another hill, Golgotha—only Moses and Elijah don't appear on this hill. Two thieves hang on either side of him.

The church's word for this experience is *transfiguration*. As God's glory shone upon Jesus, he was changed into a person of light. That's the way it is with God's glory; it changes everything it touches. Someday, by the grace of God, you and I will also shine with that same glory.

Jesus' transfiguration glory was a foreshadowing of his resurrection glory, a vision given to the disciples to let them know they were on the right track. It was a story the disciples told over and over again to help them persevere through whatever lay ahead.

When Jesus was crucified, the disciples remembered that glorious day; how he told them that even his death would not eliminate God's glory. When they were persecuted, they remembered and believed that even their own deaths could not eliminate God's glory. They told the transfiguration story whenever they were uncertain about what they were doing and who they were following, and they believed in the glory of God even though they could not always see it.

We are also asked to believe in the glory of God when we are stuck in darkness. In situations like that, all we have is the transfiguration story, the belief that Jesus and the disciples were changed by God's glory, and that someday we will be too. Stories are powerful things if you decide to believe in them. Because we believe in the transfiguration story, we live in a different world, a world where glory is always possible.

Suffering and death do not have the final word. Glory and light are the last words. Terrible things still happen. Suffering, doubt, despair, and death are very real, and they frighten us, but we believe they are not all there is. We believe that the light of God's glory can break out and change our darkest times. We believe in a world where, like Sandy Ballard, in any given moment, you can walk down the street, turn the corner, hear the voice of God, and be forever changed.

SUGGESTIONS FOR WORSHIP

Call to Worship

LEADER: The mighty One, God the Lord, speaks and summons the earth from the rising of the sun to its setting.

PEOPLE: **Out of Zion, the perfection of beauty, God shines forth.**

LEADER: Our God comes and does not keep silence; before God is a devouring fire, and a mighty tempest all around.

PEOPLE: **God calls to the heavens above and to the earth, that God may judge the people.**

LEADER: Let us worship the God of righteousness.

Ash Wednesday

Vicki G. Lumpkin

Joel 2:1-2, 12-17: The prophet foretells the day of the Lord and calls the people to return with rent hearts to receive mercy.

Psalm 51:1-17: The psalmist pleads for God's mercy, seeking a new heart and a right spirit.

2 Corinthians 5:20*b*–6:10: God's faithful servants "have nothing, and yet possess everything."

Matthew 6:1-6, 16-21: Jesus' teachings on prayer and fasting.

REFLECTIONS

The texts for Ash Wednesday convey themes of both judgment and hope. Together, they call believers to heartfelt repentance, and for all who return to God, they offer promises of restoration and forgiveness. The texts locate the root of genuine holiness in an inner transformation that leads to new ways of relating both to God and to others.

The Gospel text assumes believers will engage in acts of piety, but calls for careful probing of the underlying reasons for performing them. Using the acts of almsgiving, prayer, and fasting as examples, the Gospel writer excoriates the public displays of praise-seeking "hypocrites" while admonishing believers to perform such acts in humility and secrecy. The temporal rewards of human adulation are contrasted with the rewards of divine approval, a treasure that "neither moth nor rust consumes and [which] thieves do not break in and steal." The passage calls for a careful consideration of the idea of secondary gain: What is our motivation and what personal benefit do we derive from such acts of faithfulness?

The passage from Matthew demands self-examination, particularly when placed in the Lenten context: Are our practices truly acts of faithfulness, or are they in some way acts of self-service? What inner transformation must occur to bring us to the point where we cherish the incorruptible approbation of God above all else? What changes must we make in our lives in order to set our sights and hearts on such a heavenly treasure?

A SERMON BRIEF

Seeking a Rave Review

Anthropologists suggest that in our distant past, religion and theater shared common roots. On this first day of Lent, the Gospel text takes us to the world of the theater for instruction in Christian living, to the place of trumpet fanfares, audiences, and masks.

Our Gospel text comes from the Sermon on the Mount, a speech given by Jesus beginning in Matthew 5 and continuing through chapter 7. The passage contains practical advice for Christian living. In this passage, Jesus contrasts the "hypocrites" with the righteous. "Hypocrites" is a Greek word, a term that means "actors," people who get up on stage and play a role. In the world of the theater, not everything is as it appears. Stage props and scenery may look like the real thing, but up close they can be seen for what they really are: fakes. In the theater, not everything is as it appears, but appearances are everything. There are two things actors take seriously: their art and their reviews. Most actors keep scrapbooks of their reviews. Good reviews promote careers, and what the critics say can make or break a production. Good reviews mean big audiences, and the audience is primary, for without the eye of the beholder, there is no theater.

Although the audience may be primary in the theater, as Christians the temptation to play to the spectator is the very thing we are told to resist. With wonderful hyperbole, Jesus tells us to avoid the fanfare and forgo the performance. The acts of the Christian life, he tells us, are not props to be used for self-promotion and ego enhancement. In fact, they are not to be turned into acts—performances—at all. They are rightly done in humility and genuineness, and in such privacy that we ourselves are barely cognizant of their accomplishment. Instead of being fodder for human adulation, they are the food of our spirits. For this reason he cautions against turning the temple of our spirits into a stage for public performance.

There are three examples of Christian disciplines in this passage: almsgiving, the act of giving to those in need; prayer, the act of communicating directly with God; and fasting, choosing not to eat in order to devote more time to prayer. Other examples could have been used, perhaps the study of Scripture or participating in corporate worship. The issue is not the activities; the text assumes that we will engage in such things. What is being examined is our motivation. The point is not whether we pray or give alms or fast, but how and why we do it. Do we do it because we are seeking human praise and attention? Or is our primary goal deepening our spirituality and glorifying God? The text reminds us there are two kinds of rewards, temporary and enduring. The question inherent in the text plumbs the allegiance of our heart: What is it that we truly treasure? Will we stroke our egos or build our spirits? Will we seek human approval or Divine? We are asked to face a fact that every actor knows: at some point the echoes of human applause will dissipate.

In Dallas, there is a new church that worships in a professional theater. Periodically during the performance season, the congregation serves dinner to the cast and crew, and then attends the production afterward. The fellowship meal affords an opportunity for both groups to get to know each other better. Church members are always surprised to discover the disparity between the actors' roles and their real lives. The actor who plays a calloused drug dealer in the play is the same person who will be defending his dissertation on counseling next week; the middle-aged woman who plays the owner of a raunchy bar is active in her local church and in a variety of social causes; the struggling and hungry young actress is arrogant and filthy rich on stage. The friendly people who gather in the theater kitchen become far different characters when the costumes are on, the overture begins, and the curtain goes up.

A popular maxim states that character is what we display when no one is looking. Put another way, a performer is a different person on stage than off. The Gospel of Matthew would agree. The depth of our Christianity is best measured when no one is looking and when we're not out to impress anyone. The prayers that we pray and the acts that we do in solitude, away from the spectators, give the full measure of our faith. That is why God sets such high value on them. The point of this passage, however, is that no deed is ever performed outside of God's vision. Jesus tells us three times, "Your Father who sees in secret will reward you."

Jesus' message is that God is not oblivious to what we do in private. The prayers, the fasting, the almsgiving, the study, the unseen acts of ministry and compassion, things others might overlook, are noticed by a watchful, caring God. Not only noticed, but acknowledged, rewarded. Best of all, implied in such acts is a relationship. God is engaged with us, whether we are in public or in solitude. Doing these things simply for the sake of pleasing God and no one else reaps the blessing of deepening the relationship. This is the treasure that endures.

This Ash Wednesday text and the Lenten journey itself call us to examine the various roles we play and our motivation for playing them. Particularly with respect to our Christianity, we are called to disavow acting in favor of authenticity.

Truthfully, we will probably never make the pages of *Variety* because of our devotional practices, whether public or private. Particularly if practiced in obscurity, our prayers and good deeds will never garner the approbation of our friends and neighbors. Nor should they, according to this passage. Jesus tells us that there is only one critique worth seeking, and that is the rave review inherent in the words, "Well done, thou good and faithful servant" (Matt. 25:21 KJV).

SUGGESTIONS FOR WORSHIP

Call to Worship

ONE:	Blow the trumpet and call a solemn assembly!
ALL:	**Gather the people and sanctify the congregation!**
ONE:	Let us return to the Lord with single-minded purpose.
ALL:	**Let us be reconciled to our God.**
ONE:	Then will God remove our sin,
ALL:	**And our hearts will be restored.**
ONE:	For our God is gracious and merciful,
ALL:	**Slow to anger and abounding in steadfast love.**

Prayer of Confession

Merciful God, we confess that it is easier to wear ashes than to truly humble ourselves. We would rather fast than feed the poor. We would rather put on sackcloth than cover the naked. We would rather offer eloquent prayers than work for justice. We ask your forgiveness for accepting the path of easy piety. Create in us a new and right spirit that we might follow the way of Jesus on the journey of true discipleship. Amen.

Assurance of Pardon

ONE: Our assurance of pardon is found in the words of the psalmist: "The sacrifice acceptable to God is a broken spirit; a broken and contrite heart, O God, you will not despise."

ALL: **By God's grace, we are forgiven.**

Benediction

May the Lenten quest on which you now embark
bring you to places of restoration and wholeness.
May it bring you to new heights of devotion and discipleship,
and may the reward you seek and find
be the treasure of God's love and blessing.

First Sunday in Lent

Gail Anderson Ricciuti

Genesis 9:8-17: God makes a covenant, marked by the sign of the rainbow, with Noah and all creation.

Psalm 25:1-10: The psalmist seeks knowledge of God's ways.

1 Peter 3:18-22: As Noah and his family were saved through water, God now saves us through the waters of baptism representing the life, death, and resurrection of Jesus Christ.

Mark 1:9-15: After his baptism by John, Jesus is driven into the desert to endure the temptation, and then returns to proclaim the good news of the kingdom of God.

REFLECTIONS

Baptism, relegated in the consciousness of many to an innocuous rite of membership, is in reality our "watershed." As Lent begins, the church commences its inexorable march with Jesus toward Jerusalem. He turns in the direction of the city and everything it represents; and it is baptism that sets *us* in the same direction. Mark uses a kind of hallmark "shorthand" that is not mere chronology: within just six nuance-laden verses, baptism, temptation, and ministry are all tied together.

Considering the Spirit's forceful action, it is evident that "wilderness" is not only located on the plains of Judea. And baptism, rather than guaranteeing spiritual armament, is seemingly the act that strips armor away and lays the baptized open to beast no less than to ministering angels. If we are protected, it is not by virtue of any ritual or rite, but only by the same Spirit that urgently "drives" us out of our comfort zone.

A SERMON BRIEF
Wild Beasts and Angels

On Canada's Baffin Island lies a starkly beautiful wilderness some six hundred miles beyond the tree line. Its name is Auyuittuq; in the

Inuit tongue, "the land that never melts." Some years ago, at the time my husband Anthony and I backpacked into its rugged valley, it was still the farthest northern national park on earth.

Before they allow you to hike into Auyuittuq, the rangers require you to attend an orientation to the landscape, to your responsibility for your own safety, but most of all to polar bears. Ordinarily during the brief arctic summer, the polar bears remain at the upper end of the island, where the ice never entirely goes out; but once in a great while a bear will wander down the sixty miles of glacial valley in search of food. Consequently, after reminding you that you are six hundred miles north of the nearest tree, the rangers give you a short course in polar bear defense: simply drop your pack between you and the bear, and begin to back away. ("But," I was thinking, "there is nothing to back away *to!*")

At the end of orientation they make you sign a waiver: "I will not hold the national park liable for my accidental death or catastrophic injury. I understand the only defense against a polar bear is a rifle; and I affirm that I am not carrying firearms of any kind into the park."

Mark sketches the details of Jesus' emergence from the Jordan as if to say that baptism, your "adventure orientation" to the life ahead, is a little like that. You sign a kind of divine waiver, abandoning your *non*involvement with principalities and powers, and signing a surety of beasts and angels.

Many parents somehow believe that they should "get the baby done" as early as possible for protection, when, in reality, Mark implies that baptizing is dangerous business. Perhaps we should think twice about plunging right in (forgive the pun), when baptism will make us more vulnerable, rather than less.

You end up in the wilderness—because the Spirit drives you there! Not Satan, notice, but the Holy Spirit—the same Spirit who is with you from the beginning because you are in the image of God, the same Spirit who breathes the spark of life into you when you are naked and wailing, and who graces you in an even fuller way when you are baptized. What this may mean for believers is that wilderness is *not* a place of death, but it is still wild—there are beasts—and there are angels.

Although other Gospel writers go on in detail about *how* Satan met Jesus, Mark's words are spare. No devilish wiliness is described; Mark implies simply that the newly baptized Jesus is pressed to his limits. This postbaptismal time is the crucible of Jesus' ministry—just as it is for us. And the voice that speaks to him is the same for us as well: "[This is] my beloved—in whom I am well pleased" (KJV). All of this would seem to say that wilderness is not the punishment we often think it is. Instead, what if it is precisely *because* God is well pleased with you that you are driven to a place where you are fair game for beasts and angels?

At his baptism, Jesus is prepared to launch a ministry beholden to none of the former assumptions of the religious establishment, nor to the political establishment personified by Caesar's occupying forces. We watch his progression from water to wilderness to word: "The time is fulfilled, and the kingdom of God has come near; repent, and believe in the good news."

In the popular mind, Lent is usually associated with giving things up. It is assumed that you get baptized, you "get religion," you are separated out and turned away from worldly cravings when, in fact, the movement is in the opposite direction. We face "wild beasts," the common language of the prophets when speaking of ultimate things. It is not self-denial, but a taking on of things—a shouldering of commitments—*because* we renounce obligation to the consumerist, militarist, and patriarchal values of our culture.

Instead of seeing Satan as some personal devil, we encounter Satan as the essence of systems and structures that lock people in poverty, in pettiness, in half-light. Into those places is precisely where we must journey—if indeed wilderness is the crucible of our ministry.

What are your beasts? Which ones circle you, stalk you, call you on your cell phone out on the highway—or simply sit down and debate you as you go about your work in the classroom, courtroom, boardroom, nursery, or office?

And what is your wilderness—a bothersome place from which to extricate yourself as quickly as possible, or the rootbed of your ministry?

And who are the angels whose very presence enables you to go on? By whose remembrance or voice, presence or touch, are you ministered to when there is not a safe tree in sight to climb if you could?

Genesis tells us that God's covenant is established with every living thing, with beasts as well as human beings. Perhaps being loved by our earthly angels teaches us that even the beasts are kindred flesh; what most frightens us is something to which we are akin. And the way we handle the beasts is being watched by the angels. "I affirm that I am entering the wilderness without weapons."

As Lent commences its long march through our lives, remember your baptism—which did not make you safe, but made you for this time a wilderness wanderer. May both the beasts and the angels with whom you live bless the journey!

SUGGESTIONS FOR WORSHIP

Call to Worship (based on Genesis 9:8-17)

LEADER: People of faith, God has established a covenant with us, with all who went before us, and with our descendants after us.

PEOPLE: God's covenant is with every living creature of the earth.

LEADER: Since we are promised that the earth shall never again be destroyed,

PEOPLE: We too are bound to keep covenant with God.

LEADER: Because the God of Noah remembers, let us who are servants of Christ remember.

ALL: We will honor the covenant by offering our worship and praise!

Prayer of Confession
(based on Psalm 25:1-7 and 1 Peter 3:18, 21)

LEADER: All the paths of the Lord are steadfast love and faithfulness, for those who keep covenant with God. Friends, because there is no one who has not stumbled from the path, let us appeal to God for a good conscience.

ALL: To you, O Lord, we lift up our souls. God of our salvation, be mindful of your mercy and your steadfast love, for they have been from of old. Do not remember the sins of our youth or our transgressions; according to your steadfast love remember us, for your goodness' sake, O Lord! [Silent prayers of confession.]

LEADER: O God, in you we trust.

PEOPLE: Do not let us be put to shame.

Assurance of Pardon

LEADER: These are true words that we can trust: "For Christ also suffered for sins once for all, the righteous for the

unrighteous, in order to bring you to God." My
friends, hear and believe the good news of the gospel:

ALL: **In Jesus Christ, we are forgiven!**

Benediction

Go now to walk among beasts and angels, surrounded by a peace
the world cannot give. And may the God who, in Christ, has walked
the way before you, accompany you in every step. Amen.

Second Sunday in Lent

Elaine G. Siemsen

Genesis 17:1-7, 15-16: God's affirmation to Abram that God is powerful and faithful to those who are obedient.

Psalm 22:23-31: God remembers those who are poor, helpless, or despised. Even those who are rich and have enough will bow down to God, because God has saved them.

Romans 4:13-25: Paul interprets the actions of Abraham as a model for all who follow. Believers must not waver in their faith. God raised Jesus so that we would be acceptable to God.

Mark 8:31-38: Jesus tells of his suffering and death, rebukes Peter, calls the disciples, and gives added meaning for a life of sacrifice and obedience.

REFLECTIONS

The initial reading of the Gospel text draws one's attention to Peter's rejection of Jesus' view of the future. Certainly preaching parallels can be drawn between Peter's confession found in Mark 8:29 and his rejection of Jesus' death in 8:32. This is a familiar preaching setting in Lent, where the sermon often focuses on the human condition that rejects Jesus almost as swiftly as Peter. This first section of the text clearly amplifies a Lenten theme of human failing.

However, there is a second theme that sounds clearly in the text. This is Jesus' call to discipleship. In this passage, the hearer is confronted by Jesus inviting the crowd to accept the task of a mission in the world. This alternative theme allows preaching that draws attention to discipleship and refocuses the hearers' attention upon serving the Christ, away from the frequent Lenten refrain of self-criticism.

Second, this theme of discipleship that pursues the idea of the mission of the church gives the preacher the opportunity to link together

59

several texts from the Gospel of Mark. Three texts that blend well on this theme are 6:8-9, 3:35, and 8:34. In all of these, Mark tells the reader that to be a disciple of Jesus means to:

a. Take nothing with you into the world (6:8-9);
b. Do the will of God (3:35);
c. Accept that death may be a necessary part of the mission (8:34).

As Jesus moves toward the cross with its promise of resurrection, Mark's structure and themes move the hearer away from the response of Peter, motivated by self-interest and fear, and toward a confident response that answers Christ's call to serve. The preacher has the opportunity to encourage hearers to use this Lenten season to explore their own calls to discipleship.

The construction of the sermon could go in two different directions. A narrative style sermon that links together the Marcan texts that are mentioned above would give focus to the theme of "Mission Possible." This narrative sermon might tell the story of the disciples trying to understand how these three teachings fit together. The sermon might be based on a fictional character, a member of the crowd who is fitting this message of discipleship into his or her life.

An inductive sermon would also work well with this text. Jesus calls all hearers of the gospel to a disciple's life that is focused on mission to the world. The sermon might start with the assumption that the hearers are willing to be disciples, but are unclear as to how to start. Peter's rejection might be the example of a bad first impression for a new disciple of Jesus.

A SERMON BRIEF

The words of Jesus always seem foolish to me. Why should I think about taking up the cross? Life does a really good job of placing crosses on my back and in my path. I do not need to seek them out. Taking up the cross means adding burdens to my already overwhelming life! Taking up the cross means having all my failures brought to light for others to critique.

Many of us have heard sermons over the years that have encouraged us to carry the additional burden that is the cross. Maybe carrying the cross was identified with illness or poverty or some other personal burden. Your response may have been much like mine—and the apostle Peter's. This burden will bring more pain, more suffering, into my life or the lives of those I love. Like Peter, we often reject Jesus' request. We cannot accept any more burdens—especially not the cross. Like the disciples, we choose to avoid this unpleasant subject. This burden symbolizes an extraordinary sacrifice. Taking up our cross means that we must now "make right" all these errors and mistakes in our past. Taking up the burden of the cross means punishing ourselves, making our lives more difficult, more depressing, more unpleasant.

But this is not what Jesus is saying! Jesus is not demanding that we add burdens to ourselves. In fact, when Jesus invites us to take up our cross, he is telling us to unburden ourselves. In Mark 6, Jesus says, "Take nothing with you." One way that I can take up my cross for Christ is to leave all of my concerns for myself behind. I can stop focusing my attention on my mistakes, my failures, my desires, or my wants. The cross directs my attention outside of myself. When I take up the cross, I am free to carry the hope and love of Christ. This is Christ's gift of the cross. When I give up carrying all of my own grievances, such as family members who have disappointed me, or lack of the money or recognition that I desire, I will be freed.

Taking up the cross, Jesus teaches in Mark 3:35, means that we will seek out the will of God. As we take up our crosses, we look at others, seeking, like Jesus, to understand the fears and hardships in their lives. We experience God's will as the call to minister to those who have little or who are oppressed by the social, political, or religious structures of our families and communities. Taking up the cross gives me the strength to see that many others are truly powerless to free themselves from oppression, and that I can offer them help. When we seek God's will, we see the child who needs a mentor, the aged who need love, the poor who need a share of our wealth.

Finally, taking up our cross means that we find the ways to challenge the oppressors of the world. In Mark 8:38, we learn that this may mean endangering ourselves as we confront evil that oppresses others. On a personal level, this might mean finally facing the family member whose substance abuse has controlled and oppressed the family for years. This might mean supporting the local food pantry or homeless shelter within our community. This might mean speaking out on behalf of local youths who need adult support and guidance.

Taking up the cross of Christ is an invitation to open up our lives. It is an invitation to redefine ourselves. Carrying the cross will lessen our tendencies to be full of our own life's dramas. The weight of the cross will remind us to fill up our lives with the needs of others. Taking up our cross means that our needs, desires, and fears are no longer the primary motivator for all that we do. Our energies, our decisions, our causes will now be motivated by the desire to remove fear from the faces of others.

Jesus invites us to find freedom in taking up the cross—freedom from ourselves, freedom to live out the hope and compassion that God sends to us in the life, death, and resurrection of Jesus the Christ.

SUGGESTIONS FOR WORSHIP

Prayer of Confession/Assurance of Pardon

LEADER: We gather together in community to speak aloud our fears and failings. We come trusting that God stands among us offering forgiveness and hope. Creator God, Jesus calls us to take up the cross and carry it into the world.

ALL: **We cannot lift the cross when our eyes see only our own burdens.**

LEADER: Redeemer God, Jesus calls us to take up the cross and carry it into the world.

ALL: **We cannot walk with the cross when we are hiding in fear, away from the problems of the world.**

LEADER: Sanctifying God, Jesus calls us to take up the cross and carry it into the world.

ALL: **We cannot speak of the power of the cross to heal and bring hope when we refuse to see the oppression within our families, our communities, and our world.**

Gracious God, help us diminish our own concerns, calm our fears, and open our eyes so that we can carry the cross into our families, communities, and world. Give us the strength to proclaim to all the power of Christ to heal and bring hope.

LEADER: God who created us, redeems us, and sanctifies us has heard our cries. God comes to us in Jesus Christ, our crucified and risen Lord, to give us the strength to pick up our cross and carry it into the world.

ALL: **Amen.**

Third Sunday in Lent

Katherine Thomas Paisley

Exodus 20:1-17: The Ten Commandments are God's guide to living according to God's plan, which bring blessing and peace to all who follow them.

Psalm 19: Creation proclaims the glory of God, and the law of God is a precious gift to us, through which we are blessed.

1 Corinthians 1:18-25: God's wisdom seems foolish to the world, and we are saved through the "foolishness" of the cross.

John 2:13-22: When Jesus finds people abusing the Temple by trading, he is furious and creates a scene. His prophetic words concerning his resurrection are misunderstood.

REFLECTIONS

Although the Ten Commandments are familiar to many of us, they may be *so* familiar that we no longer hear them clearly. Perhaps we need to hear the words of Deuteronomy 11:26-28 as a preface, "See, I am setting before you today a blessing and a curse: the blessing, if you obey the commandments of the LORD your God that I am commanding you today; and the curse, if you do not obey the commandments of the LORD your God, but turn from the way that I am commanding you today, to follow other gods that you have not known." We might listen better if we are reminded of what is at stake.

It is not that we believe that God goes around with a tally card for each person, like in a miniature golf game, rattling off curses if our score is too high. Rather, in the Ten Commandments, God offers us the hidden wisdom on which creation is based: the boundaries which, when respected, will enable us to live safely and happily. If we ignore the boundaries, we will find our families broken, a growing disparity between rich and poor in our communities, and a loss of

63

meaning in our culture—not because God wills it so—but because that is what happens when we ignore the behaviors, and the boundaries, which are in our best interest.

Just in case we think we might know some people, communities, and nations with some of these boundary-related problems, 1 Corinthians 1:18-25 has some suggestions on how to turn things back around. We need to rethink what we consider wisdom and foolishness.

A SERMON BRIEF

An Alternate Vision

Any parent, teacher, or youth leader knows that presentation matters. "Slave Day" will be less popular with teens than "Rent-a-Youth"; choices between two outfits for a two-year-old may stave off a tantrum at the idea of getting dressed. So instead of rebelling against the dictates of authority, just for today let's think of the Decalogue as "God's Guidelines for a Happy Life." After all, a loving God wouldn't want us to live in a country where we didn't know the rules!

Guidelines one through four have to do with underlying priorities. Basically, they tell us that we will be happier if we remember who is God (God, Yahweh, the Lord) and who is not (us). Thinking that we are in charge leads to frustration, disillusionment, disregard of the needs of others, and ultimately even despair. Guideline two advises us that we will be more in tune with ourselves and all of creation if we worship the Lord rather than what we have done, or another person, or our children. Putting our careers first, or compromising our values in order to make money are very destructive for persons and society—and God, who loves us, wants better for us than that. Worshiping only God helps keep the rest of life in perspective. We are to speak of God respectfully. That too shows our priorities, as does allowing one day to stop and worship God, and reflect on our blessings. In the midst of the confusion of life, a day to get our heads on straight sounds like a good idea! Time-management expert Stephen Covey, who tries to help us get our priorities straight, puts this advice in our own idiom, but guidelines one through four urge us to "keep first things first."

The remaining six guidelines support good relationships in our families and communities. Honoring parents prevents arrogance, even in the teen years and early adulthood when we may think our parents have nothing worthwhile to offer us. Not committing murders would free our communities from fear and prejudices. Adultery-free relationships offer more security, and less brokenness. Not stealing helps build community trust, concern for others, and enables more giving. Truth in the courts would tend to foster justice. Not coveting what belongs to another would make for good relationships and general contentment with one's own life—surely a good thing. Perhaps getting back to these basics would be a better program for social reform than anything on the docket of Congress.

What is so appealing is that these divine guidelines speak to our internal longings, when we are still enough to listen. We all long for homes in which we are respected and cherished. We long for communities in which our children can play safely in the streets, our businesses are respected and without risk of burglary, and where we are a part of a just society. Together, they present an alternate vision of how we might live, pointing to God's design for our lives, which offers ways to fulfill God's intentions for us and gives us the inner security for which we dream. The right boundaries provide both safety and peace of mind. Years ago, some psychologists thought that fences around playgrounds were negative influences, so they took them down. The children had total freedom—no boundaries, no fences. But when the boundaries were removed, the children did not run freely through the area as they had previously. They stayed in the center of the playground, and indicated feelings of insecurity at leaving that limited area. When the fences were replaced, they again used the entire playground—right up to the fenced edges. Security was restored with the fences! Boundaries help give shape to our lives, and help us fulfill the potential within us.

The problem is that these divine guidelines, however much they appeal to our inner nature, challenge the cultural assumptions in which we live. "More is better." "It isn't wrong if you don't get caught." "He who dies with the most toys wins." "If it feels good, do it." Rarely does advertising encourage, "Thinking of other people's needs will help you sleep better at night," or "Tell your family how much you love them today," or "Family dinners, not fast food, build relationships." So how do we fight the world around us?

Start with the basics. Surround yourselves with God's truth. First Corinthians reminds us that the wisdom of God seems like foolishness to the world. We live with right-side-up priorities in the midst of an upside-down world. It isn't very comfortable, but we need to remember who is right side up! We need to embrace the role of the little boy in Hans Christian Andersen's story "The Emperor's New

Clothes." After all the adults around had been told that only the wise could see the clothes, they all exclaimed of their beauty. It took the free clarity of a child to point out that the emperor was really naked!

To keep our own right-side-up perspective, we can begin the day by reading some Scripture to center our thoughts on God. When we feel conflicted through the day, we can take a time-out and spend some time in prayer. Give thanks at every meal. End the day with time together as a family, including dinner together and devotions. Pray together as a family. Take time daily to read books that nurture the soul. Breathe deeply. Laugh often. Love beyond reason—like Christ, who loved without limits. Celebrate life as a gift from God. There is no law against these things. They can be done.

The inscription on the Bok Tower outside Orlando, Florida, has these words by John Burroughs, "I come here to find myself; it is so easy to get lost in the world." These pithy words uphold God's expectations rather than our own. They reveal great insight into human frailty and our need for freedom—and they come as a gift—by the loving grace of God to a lost and confused people. AGAIN.

SUGGESTIONS FOR WORSHIP

Call to Worship

LEADER: We gather as God's people, in the world, but not of the world.

PEOPLE: **Help us focus on you, Lord.**

LEADER: Speak to your people, Lord, that we might follow you.

PEOPLE: **Open our ears to hear and our minds to follow the way of truth. Amen.**

Litany (from Psalm 19:7-11 RSV)

LEADER: The law of the LORD is perfect, reviving the soul;

PEOPLE: **The testimony of the LORD is sure, making wise the simple;**

LEADER: The precepts of the LORD are right, rejoicing the heart;

PEOPLE: **The commandment of the LORD is pure, enlightening the eyes;**

LEADER: The fear of the LORD is clean, enduring for ever;

PEOPLE: **The ordinances of the LORD are true, and righteous altogether.**

LEADER:	More to be desired are they than gold, even much fine gold;
PEOPLE:	**Sweeter also than honey and drippings of the honeycomb.**
LEADER:	Moreover by them is thy servant warned;
PEOPLE:	**In keeping them there is great reward.**

Music Notes

Traditional hymns: "A Charge to Keep I Have"; "O God, Our Help in Ages Past"; "Be Thou My Vision"

Contemporary music: "The Basics of Life" by Mark Harris and Don Koch (recorded by 4HIM); "I Will Stand" by Pam Thum, Joel Lindsey, Regie Hamm, and Cliff Downs (recorded by Pam Thum)

Fourth Sunday in Lent

Loretta Reynolds

Numbers 21:4-9: The Israelites grumble against Moses in the wilderness, experience God's wrath in the form of poisonous serpents, and are granted deliverance by means of the bronze serpent lifted in their midst.

Psalm 107:1-3, 17-22: The people of Israel recall their ancestors' experience of God's faithfulness and sing praise to God for God's saving acts.

Ephesians 2:1-10: We have been saved by God's grace in Jesus Christ, not by any doing of our own.

John 3:14-21: The bronze serpent lifted by Moses in the wilderness is replaced by the sacrifice of Christ as the ultimate sign of God's redeeming grace.

REFLECTIONS

Jesus' life and death is the perfect portrait of God's self-giving love. Through Jesus, God provides a picture of how grace and forgiveness supersede law and judgment. Fullness of life originates in God and is freely offered to every person. This salvation is not only a past event, but also a present experience and a future hope. Salvation is a call to a life of good works. These good works are the outcome, not the cause, of salvation. Thus, belief in Jesus will be reflected in a life of service to others.

A SERMON BRIEF

A Portrait of Love

What does love look like to you? Perhaps it is a family game of basketball or the smudged face of a toddler after a day of making mud

68

pies. Maybe love is the picture of a parent cooking breakfast, or a child practicing the piano. I can still see my father making a total check of my car before allowing me to head back to college. Then I thought it was a delay tactic—now I know it was love. The memory of walking with my husband along a moonlit beach in Australia, thank-you notes from students, an E-mail from a friend half a world away—all are portraits of love. I wonder, what does love look like to you?

After graduating from college, I worked in the Caribbean for two years, where I provided after-school activities for children. I decided to follow my vacation Bible school tradition and served cookies and punch every afternoon. Each day the children would take the three cookies that they were allowed, but instead of eating them they would wrap them in handkerchiefs and put them in their book bags. After a few days, my curiosity got the best of me, and I asked, "Why?" I remember one little girl in particular. She gave me the most puzzled look and then a simple explanation: "I have two little sisters at home." It took me a minute to catch on, but you see, these children could not imagine eating a special treat like a cookie and not sharing it with the rest of the family. Sometimes love looks like cookies, punch, and little children.

Portraits of self-giving love can be heartwarming and restful to the eye. But other pictures of self-sacrificial love can be heartrending and disturbing to the soul. God's self-giving nature is seen in Jesus' life of love and forgiveness. We call it the gospel. Look again at this beautifully familiar picture. (Read John 3:14-17.)

Sometimes true love looks like a cross. The truth of the matter is this: believing in Jesus is not a recipe for an easy life. When we believe in Jesus, we buy into Jesus' way of life. He didn't just talk about self-giving love—he lived it. Selfless love can get you in a lot of trouble.

Eula Hall is not a doctor or a lawyer or a government official. She is a woman who grew up in rural poverty. She has been threatened and discouraged, but she never gave up. Not long ago I listened to this remarkable woman tell about her life. More than thirty years ago Eula decided that rather than just being depressed about the terrible health conditions of the people in her home area, she would do something about it. She believed that health care was a human right, not a privilege. She had watched too many friends and neighbors suffer and die because they were too poor to afford lifesaving medicine. She was only one person, but she was determined to do something to provide health care for this rural area. And do something she did.

She moved out of her house and turned it into a clinic. She lobbied Congress, wrote grant applications, argued with government officials, and raised money any way she could. In 1970, a new Mud Creek clinic was built. It has now expanded to include dental care, a food pantry, a clothes closet, and Social Security assistance. When Eula sees a need, she responds. When she realized that many people were not receiving their proper benefits from government agencies because they couldn't afford lawyers, she learned how to represent them in court. And even though she is more than seventy years old, when the ambulance refuses to travel down many of the mountain roads to pick up someone who is sick, Eula goes to them in her four-wheel-drive vehicle. If a person can't pay for medicine, Eula takes care of it. She is one amazing woman. And for me, that is the wonder of it all. She is one person who decided to do something. And her "doing something" has saved or increased the quality of life for thousands. Now that is a portrait of self-giving love!

Eula will quickly tell you that God is the one who gives her the strength to go on. She is painfully aware that doing what is right is not always easy nor is it always popular. She has withstood ridicule, she has gone without many things that she desired so that others could have the basics, and people have even shot at her. Living a life of self-giving love is not easy and often not appreciated by others.

Frankly, we are uncomfortable with heroes and prophets like Eula. They make us nervous because they call us to be more than we are. They will not let us be content with injustice. Peter Gomes observed, "It is easier to honor the dead than to follow the living." What a powerful and true statement! Isn't that often the way we relate to Jesus? We can honor him because he is no longer among us, upsetting our settled lives with his ideals of forgiveness and grace. It's easier to honor and worship the Jesus who sits on a heavenly throne than to follow the living Jesus in a way of life that led to a cross.

Jesus' obedience to God's self-giving love is what got him in trouble. He was killed because of the way he lived. In his living he touched the untouchables, sheltered the homeless, gave dignity to those who were hurting, fed and clothed the poor, listened to those who were shunned by society, and invited both saints and sinners to dine at his table. You would think this kind of love and inclusiveness would make him the most popular person around, but no, that much love makes us uncomfortable. That portrait is too real, too messy, too demanding. Looking into that mirror hurts too much, for it reflects our own distortion and ugliness, and so they killed that love. If he had only changed his lifestyle, if he had only let up a little on the "love your enemy stuff" and had stopped hanging out with all the riffraff, maybe things could have been different. But regardless of the danger he brought upon himself, he remained obedient to God's call upon his life. With determination and compassion he remained obedient to living a life that was the representation of God's self-giving love in human form. Jesus was God's ultimate portrait of love.

Being obedient to God is about doing what we can to ensure justice and dignity for all of God's children. Choosing to follow God is about loving those who may make your life miserable. Believing in God is about standing for those who cannot stand, and speaking for those who cannot speak—even if what you must say goes against the status quo. Living an obedient lifestyle is not easy or glamorous. But that is the way of Jesus. Do we dare join Jesus in living the kind of life that puts us on the road to the cross?

So, as our Lenten journey progresses and we draw very near to the cross, what does love look like to you? What kind of portrait will you paint with your life?

SUGGESTIONS FOR WORSHIP

Call to Worship

ONE:	O give thanks to the Lord, for God is good;
ALL:	**God's steadfast love endures forever.**
ONE:	Your steadfast love is higher than the heavens,
ALL:	**and your faithfulness reaches to the clouds.**
ONE:	O give thanks to the Lord, for God is good!

Prayer of Confession and Assurance of Pardon

RIGHT:	**O God, when we become proud, remind us,**
LEFT:	It is your grace that saves us.
RIGHT:	**When we become arrogant and self-assured, remind us,**
LEFT:	Life is a gift from you.
RIGHT:	**When we strive and struggle and boast of our accomplishments, remind us,**
LEFT:	We are only what you made us to be.

RIGHT: **When we become self-centered and self-absorbed, remind us, O God,**

LEFT: That how we love our neighbor is evidence of how we love you.

ALL: **Through the self-giving love of God, we are forgiven.**

Benediction

As you leave this place to meet the challenges of life, may you encounter God at every turn. And may you experience God's grace along every step of your journey. Amen.

Fifth Sunday in Lent

Beverly A. Zink-Sawyer

Jeremiah 31:31-34: Through the prophet Jeremiah, God promises to enter into a new, enduring covenant with the people of Israel, a covenant written on their hearts.

Psalm 51:1-12: The psalmist confesses sinfulness and implores God for a clean heart and a right spirit.

Hebrews 5:5-10: Jesus the great high priest is held forth as an example of humble obedience to God.

John 12:20-33: In response to curious Greek visitors who ask to see him, Jesus interprets his impending suffering and death.

REFLECTIONS

Something about Jesus always attracted crowds, prompting the Pharisees who monitored him to remark, at the close of the text preceding our Gospel text from John, "Look, the world has gone after him" (12:19). Whether he was performing spectacular nature-defying miracles, telling stories about the earthiness of everyday life, or simply dwelling in the moment with his faithful friends and casual passersby, there was something compelling about Jesus' presence. So it is not strange to imagine the Greek visitors to Jerusalem for the Passover feast, who are described here, seeking out the one about whom they had heard so much.

The compelling nature of Jesus continues to call both the curious and the committed. But as the words of this text—and Jesus' life and death—so clearly remind us, the way of glory is the way of the cross. The challenge set before us as would-be disciples is to follow Jesus wherever he leads, even over the thorny and rocky roads of discipleship.

A SERMON BRIEF

Not long ago, a wonderful new bookstore opened a few miles from our house. On my first visit to the sparkling new store, I headed for the "Religion" section to check out what had been designated as "religious" books. There I found the usual array of Bibles and devotional books and commentaries. But then I turned to my right and noticed a long section of bookshelves adjacent to these books on religion. Atop that huge section of books was a sign saying "Spirituality," under which were books with titles like *The Journey to Wholeness, Essential Spirituality,* and one with the subtitle *How to Make Your Dreams Come True.*

We are on a human quest, it appears, a search for fulfillment. We seek to quench some deep longing inside of us that we might not even be able to name. We want answers to the mysteries of life: mysteries such as, Why do bad things happen to good people? Where will I find peace and happiness? How can I make sense out of a seemingly senseless world?

This search for meaning and happiness, of course, is nothing new. It's as old as the gospel. John tells us in the Gospel text about some Greeks who were on a quest. Perhaps Gentile converts to Judaism, these "Greeks" had come to Jerusalem for the Passover feast. "Sir," the Greek visitors said to the disciple Philip, "we wish to see Jesus." The Gospel writer doesn't tell us anything about these curious Greeks, but we can bet they had in their minds a good idea of the Jesus they wanted to see. You know, the Jesus who turned water into wine at the wedding feast in Cana, who made the blind man see and the lame man pick up his mat and walk. They wanted to see the Jesus who fed five thousand people with five barley loaves and two fish, who walked on water and brought Lazarus back to life, who does, as preacher Barbara Brown Taylor once put it, "just your basic, oh, you know, your basic raising-the-dead kind of stuff."[1]

Whatever it was that prompted their eagerness to see Jesus, I don't think those curious Greeks—or Jesus' own disciples—were prepared for what they got: a soliloquy by Jesus about a grain of wheat dying and bearing fruit, or a lesson about losing and hating one's own life, or a voice from heaven confirming the glorification of Jesus through death. Surely this kind of talk was *not* going to bring more followers into Jesus' fold. The problem was, the Greeks who sought Jesus probably already had a good idea of the kind of Jesus they wanted to see: Jesus the therapist, Jesus the problem solver, Jesus the magnificent who could make all their dreams come true. What they got instead was the Jesus who was headed for death on a cross.

But are we any different? Hating our lives, following wherever Jesus goes, taking up the cross? This really isn't what we had in mind, either. This isn't the Jesus we want to see. Give us the gentle Jesus who healed the sick and taught multitudes in those pastoral settings beside the sea. Or show us the risen Christ, triumphant in glory with arms outstretched, trampling the powers of evil and death as depicted in all those great paintings. But in between those two images of Jesus is the Jesus we'd rather not see: the one who was despised and rejected and hung on a cross.

The more accurate question for us—as it might have been for the Greeks in this Gospel story—is *not,* Do we want to see Jesus? *Anybody* would want to see the miracle man from Galilee. The question for us is, Are we willing to follow the Jesus we see? Are we willing to see and follow the *real* Jesus—not the Jesus of health, wealth, and happiness who will make all our dreams come true, but the Jesus whose glory came through obedience, even unto death on a cross?

This coming Wednesday, April 9, is the fifty-eighth anniversary of the execution of one brave disciple who followed the real Jesus to his own cross. Dietrich Bonhoeffer was hanged at Flossenburg Prison in Germany for his participation in the Confessing Church, the Protestant community that opposed the Nazi regime. Before his imprisonment, Bonhoeffer wrote a book on the cost of discipleship, not knowing how high that cost would be for him. "If we answer the call to discipleship," Bonhoeffer wrote, "where will it lead us? What decisions and partings will it demand? To answer this question we shall have to go to [Jesus], for only he knows the answer. Only Jesus Christ, who bids us follow him, knows the journey's end."[2] Surely the end of Bonhoeffer's journey, execution in a Nazi prison camp, was not the one he would have chosen. But he, like countless others before and since, gave up his own life to follow the real Jesus.

Where is the real Jesus leading you? Is he leading you to walk into a frightening new place—a new job or relationship or responsibility? Is he leading you to walk away from what has become destructive but comfortable? Maybe he is leading you to stand up for justice, or to work for the poor and the oppressed. Perhaps he is leading you into your own valley of the shadow of death.

No, we don't know where it is we will end up when we choose to follow Jesus. We don't know what it will mean to lose our lives in order to be honored by God in heaven. Indeed, as Bonhoeffer reminded us, "only Jesus Christ . . . knows the journey's end." "But we *do* know," Bonhoeffer went on, "that it will be a road of boundless mercy. Discipleship means joy." It's hard for us to imagine that the difficult way is also the joyful way. But that's the paradox of Christian faith. For it is not the easy, comfortable way that will enable us to share in the glory promised to those who follow Christ. It is, instead, on the rough road of discipleship that we see the real Jesus who walked this way before us and now walks beside us.

The question for us this Lenten season is not, Do we want to see Jesus? The question for us is, Are we willing to follow the Jesus we see—the Jesus in whom weakness becomes strength and failures are turned to success; the Jesus who calls us to let go of everything else so that our hands are free to grasp all the goodness he is waiting to give us? "Whoever serves me must follow me," Jesus said, "and where I am, there will my servant be also." There's a command in these hard sayings of Jesus. But there's also a promise: we do not walk the road of discipleship alone, but with the One whom God has glorified and in whom we find our glory as well. Thanks be to God.

SUGGESTIONS FOR WORSHIP

Prayer of Confession (from Psalm 51)

LEADER: Have mercy on us, O God, according to your steadfast love;

PEOPLE: **According to your abundant mercy, blot out our transgressions.**

LEADER: Wash us thoroughly from our iniquity, and cleanse us from our sin.

PEOPLE: **For we know our transgressions, and our sin is ever before us.**

LEADER: Create in us clean hearts, O God, and put new and right spirits within us.

PEOPLE: **Restore to us the joy of your salvation, and sustain in us willing spirits. Amen.**

Assurance of Pardon (based on Jeremiah 31)

Hear the good news! God has made a new covenant with us, a covenant written upon our hearts rather than on tablets of stone, a covenant by which God will forgive our iniquity and remember our sin no more. Friends, in Jesus Christ, the symbol of God's new covenant, we are forgiven.

1. Barbara Brown Taylor, sermon in the Odyssey *Great Preachers I* video series.
2. Dietrich Bonhoeffer, *The Cost of Discipleship* (New York: Macmillan, 1958; reprint ed. New York: Touchstone/Simon & Schuster, 1995), 38.

Palm/Passion Sunday

Brenda C. Barrows

Liturgy of the Palms:

Mark 11:1-11: Jesus' triumphal entry into Jerusalem.

Psalm 118:1-2, 19-29: The psalmist praises "the one who comes in the name of the LORD."

REFLECTIONS

There can be a lot of smug hindsight in Palm Sunday sermons. Here is this foolish crowd, all of them miserable sinners, cheering for what they think is their earthly king, while *we* know they've got it all wrong. But have they? If the Jerusalem crowd had the particulars wrong, may they still have been right to celebrate? I believe that the text tells us to celebrate Palm Sunday's "letting loose" at the same time that we acknowledge the sober reality of the Passion that is coming.

Mark insists on the importance of "untying" (loosing) the unbroken colt in a way that anticipates the freedom with which people throw their cloaks on the ground and let loose their voices in celebration when Jesus passes by. And when he does, Jesus sees "everything." My intention in this sermon is to demonstrate that Jesus saves us with his eyes wide open to our unbroken, unruly natures. In spite of what he saw in the faces around him on his ride into Jerusalem, Jesus chose to die for humanity. And because we already received that grace, we can be confident in opening ourselves to the Lord's scrutiny today—and celebrating for all we are worth, even in the shadow of the cross.

A SERMON BRIEF

"Let It Loose!"

"You just gotta cowboy up," he said. I looked blank. "You gotta bear *down*," he said, realizing that I didn't speak the language. It was my first rodeo, a festival ominously called a "stampede," and I was a greenhorn in every respect. I was working for a local newspaper in a little Midwestern town, and they'd sent me out to interview some of the riders for a personal interest story. There was the muscular acrobatic couple who worked the evening show, and there was a gray-haired rodeo clown whose job it was to save the bull riders from being trampled or gored. And now here was this plain, lanky man in his thirties who walked with a stiff, graceful kind of care. He'd been riding broncos since he was fourteen, he said. Probably would keep on a few more years. Shrug. It's a great life.

A great life; hanging on with all you've got while a bronco tries his best to throw you. A great life; broken hips, busted jaws, life on the road, and sometimes a big payoff. He meant it. And when I asked, wide-eyed, about the pain, he didn't dismiss it. He thought about the pain for a minute, and then he spoke kindly and slowly, as if I came from another planet—which I did. "You just bear down, cowboy up, and let it loose," he said. Shrug.

I won't say I knew what he meant then, or that I know for sure now. That weekend I watched from the stands as the clock ticked down ride after ride, and all I can say is what I saw. I saw people hollering like crazy from the edges of their seats for the men who could hang on for ten seconds before they hit the dirt. And I saw the men—tiny, far-off figures on manic horses—each man with one arm down in an iron grip and the other arm raised with a dancer's grace, keeping whatever balance there was in the wide world to hang onto. I saw that—mostly from between my own fingers. I saw the ambulances lined up at the edge of the field, too, their motors running, ready to go down the road in a hurry.

If you have traveled through Lent with Jesus in Mark's Gospel, you've been on the road a lot lately, but not in any real hurry. It's been foot travel, traipsing from one town to the next with Jesus and his odd set of followers. The last stop before this was Jericho, which involved its own share of hollering over a blind man who got his sight back—thanks to his persistence, not his manners. And we have been persistent, in our own ways, following this powerful, magnetic teacher whose ways keep drawing us to him.

We feel the pull to be with him, but he keeps on sending us out. Why? Why does he need a colt *now?* We've walked all the way from Jericho, and it's only a few miles more into the city, and it's all downhill from here! But someone is mumbling something about a prophecy, something in Zechariah; something about a king. Is

Jesus the king? After what we've seen lately, nothing would surprise us.

So we are not surprised when we find a colt that we've never seen before standing by a door we've never opened, right where Jesus said it would be. We untie the halter, the way he said to do. The bystanders, a tough-looking bunch, want to know what we're up to, taking this colt that belongs to someone else. He said they would ask. And we speak the lines he gave us. *"The Lord needs it and will send it back here immediately."* And they let us go. Sweet heaven, no one has ever ridden this beast before. You can tell!

Most of us who travel with Jesus in the twenty-first century have been down this road before. A lot of us are looking for the bend in the road that leads to Good Friday. We may already have the ambulances running in the backs of our minds, and we may disapprove of the hollering, palm-waving crowd in the stands around us.

Meanwhile, the Lord is already a good hundred yards down the road ahead of us, riding his untrustworthy steed right through the noisiest, wildest parts of the crowd. The colt doesn't seem to care a bit, and there's nothing stiff or nervous about the way Jesus is riding. Sometimes he reaches out and swoops a child up from the ground for a few yards. Teenagers run along behind, dodging around their parents, and the grownups lean forward as Jesus rides past. Whoever people say Jesus is, he is not the king of the killjoys.

Jesus knows why he is here and what the road ahead of him looks like. And the road ahead is not the point right now. Right now, *it's a great life.* There's a wild little horse that's been let loose, and a happy crowd around him, and the look on Jesus' face says that he wouldn't mind spending eternity with every person here. *It's a great life,* and Jesus is looking at everything in it for all he is worth. He rides right into Jerusalem, into the heart of the city, and he goes into the Temple, and he drinks in all there is to see before he leaves for the night. And everything he sees is as important as what is coming next.

The twenty-first century knows that what comes next is deeply important. What comes next is the saving death and resurrection of our Lord, and for people of faith that is as important as the road beneath our feet. And at this moment, the road leads into Jerusalem, and Jesus looks at the whole world and sees just how good life is, and just how much there is worth saving.

This is not the time for people who love Jesus to be prim and proper and careful about smiling. It's not the time to tie up your heart at the street corner, even though you know there is a hard, sad time coming. Don't lose sight of that sad time, but just look at this great life all around us. Bear down, friends! Bear down to face the pain that is sure to come, and then—*let it loose*. Let it loose and hand it over to the one who is coming, humble and riding on a colt. Hand over your worries, your stiff back, your unruly temper, and any other burden that slows you down, and join all of us foolish people by the side of the road. If you look hard, you're bound to see him soon. *Hosanna! Blessed is the one who comes in the name of the Lord!*

SUGGESTIONS FOR WORSHIP

Call to Worship (based on Psalm 118)

ONE: O give thanks to the Lord, who is good;
         Whose mercy endures forever!
MANY: **Through the ages we come to follow the Lord.**
ONE: We come with our distress;
MANY: **The Lord answers by setting us free.**
ONE: We come with our pain and fear;
MANY: **The Lord is at my side. I will forget my fear.**
ONE: Blessed is the one who comes in the name of the Lord.
ALL: **Blessed is the Lord whose mercy shines upon us;
         Give thanks to the Lord, whose mercy endures forever.**

Prayer of Confession and Assurance of Pardon

ONE: Let us confess our sin before God and in the presence of our neighbors.
MANY: **God of mercy and compassion, we confess that our faith sometimes wears thin. We let in fear, and we burst out in anger. We give pain permission to distract us from your saving love. Forgive us, we pray, and bless us with new strength to follow where you lead us in the name of Jesus Christ.**
ONE: Friends, the sins of the entire world are no match for the saving grace that has been given to us in Jesus Christ. Hear the good news! In Jesus Christ, we are forgiven. Amen.

Holy Thursday

Beverly A. Zink-Sawyer

Exodus 12:1-4 (5-10), 11-14: The first Passover is instituted through the commandments of God given to Moses and Aaron.

Psalm 116:1-2, 12-19: Recognizing God's attentiveness, the psalmist ponders an appropriate gift to offer to God in response to God's goodness.

1 Corinthians 11:23-26: The apostle Paul relates the instruction he received from the Lord concerning the celebration of the Lord's Supper.

John 13:1-17, 31*b*-35: Gathered at a table with the disciples for a final meal before his arrest and crucifixion, Jesus washes the disciples' feet and leaves them with a new commandment to love one another as he has loved them.

REFLECTIONS

The Lord's Supper, by any name, theological interpretation, or ecclesiastical practice, stands at the center of the common life of most Christian worshiping communities. Despite that place of prominence in the church, the New Testament gives us little guidance as to exactly what this sacred act means or how it should be observed. The Gospel and Epistle texts that we read each year on the night we remember Jesus' last meal with his disciples provide some of the scant biblical material we have been given on which to base our commemorative celebrations. As if we were not confused enough about the meaning and practice of the supper, these two texts give us entirely different perspectives on that last gathering of the disciples around the table with their Lord.

However, therein lies a wonderful key to the homiletical significance of these texts. It is in the juxtaposition of the two New

82

Testament texts for Holy Thursday that a word for the church emerges. The act of self-giving, self-revealing, self-forgetting love, made manifest in Jesus' washing of his disciples' feet, as recorded in the Gospel of John, cannot be separated from the source of our ability to act in such a holy way—that source being the grace of God in Jesus Christ, which we encounter each time we gather at his table. And the commemoration of Jesus' ultimate sacrifice as symbolized in the bread broken and the wine poured can never end with our taking leave of the table feeling forgiven and self-satisfied; it must move us to similar acts of love. Humbling ourselves to give or receive the refreshing gift of washed feet, either literally or symbolically, always draws us back to the One who humbled himself—even to the point of death on a cross—and commanded us to do likewise.

Indeed, humble service without recognition of the One who provides both the strength and example for our service becomes nothing more than self-satisfying good deeds, and partaking of the bread and cup with the gathered community in the presence of God without moving beyond our personal transformation to seek the transformation of the world becomes nothing more than empty ritual. The *mandatum* to love one another as Christ has loved us calls us to recognize the inextricable relationship between lives transformed by the grace of God and lives offered in loving service.

A SERMON BRIEF

Any first-year student of church history can recite the many controversies that have torn the Christian church apart over its twenty centuries. There have been controversies concerning different understandings of the nature of Christ, the work of the church, the efficacy of the sacraments, and the pressing question of how many angels can dance on the head of a pin. In more recent years, we have argued over questions of the proper social witness of the church, what makes one eligible or ineligible for ordination, how we read the Bible, and our own pressing questions, such as whether or not the youth group should be allowed to play basketball in the newly renovated fellowship hall, and what color the new carpet in the sanctuary should be.

One debate from the early Christian centuries that *did* influence the future shape of the church was the debate over monasticism. Among the questions asked were: What should Christian community look like, and how can we best honor God through our human relationships? Is Christian commitment best expressed by entering a convent or joining a monastery, renouncing all association with the world? And if life in a community of the faithful is good, would it not be even better to withdraw from all human contact, living a solitary life to pray without ceasing and without any human or worldly distraction? These are some of the questions in the debate that raged by the fourth century.

Into what must at times have been a rather tedious discussion over the shape of monasticism, came a voice of reason—the voice of Basil, Bishop of Caesarea. Basil brought a moderating influence to the strident extremes. He spoke against the individual, ascetic life and instead pioneered monasteries based on simple, faithful Christian living. In arguing against the increasingly popular hermetic style of spirituality, Basil asked this question: "If you always live alone, whose feet will you wash?"

Basil's question cuts right to the core of Christian faith, for ours is an incarnational faith; a faith that reveals itself not just in pietistic platitudes or theoretical constructions, but in the demonstration of humble acts of love. God so loved the world that God *gave* God's only begotten Son. God didn't send us a book of church discipline, or a multivolume theological treatise—thank heavens! No. "The Word became flesh," John tells us several chapters before our text, "and 'pitched his tent' [as the Greek implies] among us" (1:14). Jesus the Christ, whose life and sacrifice we celebrate this week, came to show us how to live according to a new order of being, a new way of relating to one another. And so it's not surprising that, on the night of his betrayal, Jesus wrapped a towel around his waist, picked up a basin of water, and went around the table washing his disciples' feet. "So if I, your Lord and Teacher," Jesus told them, "have washed your feet, you also ought to wash one another's feet.... I give you a new commandment, that you love one another. Just as I have loved you, you also should love one another. By this everyone will know that you are my disciples, if you have love for one another."

Now it is our turn. The *mandatum,* the new commandment of Jesus, speaks directly to us. Whose feet will you wash? Heaven knows there are plenty of dirty and aching feet out there that call us to pick up a towel and basin, and kneel down with the refreshing water of holy kindness. There are feet that are dirty because they have no clean places to walk—trapped, as they are, in places of poverty and want. There are feet that are tired from wearying journeys of life. There are feet that are blistered and callused because they have taken it upon themselves to walk miles in someone else's shoes, or to carry burdens not even their own. And there are feet that appear to be clean, but are stained with the marks of self-righteousness and pride.

But before we take up our towels and basins, we gather at this Holy Table to remember the One whose example we follow. And a funny thing happens: as we come to the table, we look down and notice that our own feet aren't so clean either. Whose feet will you wash? And who will wash *your* feet? Come to the feast that has been prepared for us. Come and receive the cleansing, refreshing, restoring grace of our Lord and Teacher, Jesus Christ. Find your life changed, and go out and change the lives of others by the power and love of the One who first loved us. Amen.

SUGGESTIONS FOR WORSHIP

Call to Worship (adapted from Psalm 116)

LEADER: What shall we return to the Lord for all God's bounty to us?

PEOPLE: We will lift up the cup of salvation and call on the name of the Lord.

LEADER: We love the Lord who has heard our voices and our supplications.

PEOPLE: We will call on the name of the Lord as long as we live. Praise the Lord.

Prayer of Confession

Eternal God, on this holy night we gather as guests at your table of grace. We know we are not worthy to partake of the abundant gifts spread before us or equal to the task of bearing your grace to a hurting and hungry world. By your mercy, forgive us, we pray, and inspire in us the humility of Jesus our Lord who knelt down and washed the feet of those he came to save. Keep us faithful to your call to love and service in Jesus Christ, in whose name we pray. Amen.

Assurance of Pardon

The God who invites us to this holy table is the God who has heard our supplications and has redeemed us in Jesus the Christ. Believe the good news of the gospel. In Jesus Christ, we are forgiven. Amen.

Benediction

Hear again the words of Jesus: "I give you a new commandment, that you love one another. Just as I have loved you, you also should love one another. By this everyone will know that you are my disciples, if you have love for one another." And now, go out into the world in peace, living and loving as disciples of Jesus Christ.

Good Friday

Tracy Hartman

Isaiah 52:13–53:12: The story of the suffering servant.

Psalm 22: The psalmist pleas for deliverance from suffering and hostility.

Hebrews 10:16-25: God's new covenant with us gives us access to God through Christ.

or **Hebrews 4:14-16, 5:7-9:** Jesus, the Great High Priest, shares in our weaknesses and offers himself as "the source of eternal salvation."

John 18:1–19:42: The narrative of Jesus' passion and death.

REFLECTIONS

New Testament scholar Gerard Sloyan wisely reminds us that the author of today's Gospel text is concerned with the religious meanings of the events in the passion narrative, not with the events themselves. Every incident is told to either illustrate the world's disinterest in the truth, or to show the fulfillment of Scripture.[1]

This sermon brief focuses on characters whom Jesus encountered as he was condemned to death, characters who were somehow disconnected from the truth, and the ways they rejected Christ throughout the narrative. Correlation will be drawn to ways that we fail to pursue the truth and similarly reject Christ in our own lives and world. Due to the length of the Gospel passage, the reading may be divided into smaller segments as noted below. Reflection, exposition, and application follow each segment of the text.

A SERMON BRIEF

An interesting cast of characters surrounds Jesus as we read John's account of the passion narrative. As we look at the suffering and death of Christ through those characters' eyes, may we be open to the truth about ourselves and the depth of God's love for us.

(Read John 18:1-11.) Look with me into the face of Judas. See his anguish as he leaves the Passover celebration and slips out into the night. See the pain as he comes face-to-face and eye-to-eye with Jesus in the garden. See the shame and guilt as he tries to return the purse to the religious leaders. In the passion narrative, Judas is infamous for betraying Christ for a mere thirty pieces of silver. Although we are quick to judge Judas for his actions, it is likely that there have been times in each of our lives when we have put our own financial gain ahead of our service and loyalty to Christ.

Judas's actions cannot be easily excused, but some scholars believe he had deeper motivation than monetary gain. Judas was a Zealot, a member of the party that eagerly anticipated a Messiah who would become Israel's political ruler and liberator. In betraying Jesus, perhaps Judas thought he might force Jesus into conflict with and victory over the Romans, thus instituting his own kingdom.

Aren't we often like Judas in this manner, assuming we understand God's motives and plans, and seeking to implement them in our own way and time? Don't we have our own agendas that we try to coerce God into following? In the solemn moments of this day, let us reflect on how we, like Judas, may have betrayed Christ.

(Read John 18:12-25.) Now look with me into the face of Peter. See the bold confidence as he pledges to follow Jesus anywhere. See the shock and disbelief as Jesus tells him that he will deny his Master three times before the night is over. See the anguish in his eyes and feel his pain as the cock crows. Just hours ago he had promised Jesus he would lay down his life for his beloved Master. Now, he has not only lied to the woman and the crowd, but he has denied his Lord.

It is easy for us to think and to say that we will be strong and faithful in the midst of persecution. It is easy to proclaim our intentions when the way we walk is easy. As we look into the face of Peter today, may we be as stricken as he was over times when we have denied Jesus, or times when we have boasted in our own strength about the depth of our commitment to Christ. Unlike Judas, Peter was able to accept Christ's forgiveness and to forgive himself. He went on to become a strong leader in the early church. Like Peter, may we experience Christ's forgiveness. May we move past the denials and failures in our own lives to become bearers of the good news.

(Read John 18:28-38.) Take a step back now and survey the larger scene before us. The rowdy crowd has brought Jesus to Pilate, willing to go to any length to secure his execution. Yet these are the same people who will not violate ceremonial regulations and not pollute themselves by entering the Gentile praetorium. Therefore, they stand far off, thronging the doors but not crossing the threshold as they clamor and shout their bloodthirsty demands—and all this with no sense of incongruity about their own conduct. See their faces. They are full of passion and righteous indignation.

But wait—are those not our faces there in the crowd? For do we not all take pains to walk with accuracy according to recognized conventions and to abide by accepted standards while we remain blind to patent social evils crying out for justice?[2] May we reflect on ways we have rejected Christ and the nature of his ministry through the social injustices we have ignored.

(Read John 18:39–19:16*a*.) Look at the face of Pontius Pilate. One gets the impression that it is the face of a just man. At first he tried to be just in his judgment of Jesus. Three times Pilate tried to release him, but the crowd would not relent. The scene was further complicated by the fact that Pilate had a rocky relationship with the Jews. On more than one occasion they had complained to the emperor, Tiberius, about him. Finally, to keep peace in Jerusalem and to protect his own position, Pilate relented and turned Jesus over to be crucified.

Unfortunately, we are also like Pilate. If observers looked at our faces, they would say that we appear to be just and good people. But how often—as individuals and congregations, as communities and governments—have we sacrificed what we knew to be right to keep the peace and protect ourselves? How often have we washed our hands of important matters because it got too hard and our careers or reputations were at stake? Is that fear one sees lurking behind the just facade?

(Read John 19:16*b*-30.) It is almost incomprehensible to us—Jesus mocked and beaten, hanging dead on the cross. We have so insulated ourselves against the reality of death in our society that we cannot bear to look at his face and to feel what he must have felt. On this most dreadful day, during this time of reflection, may we not be like the soldiers who cast lots for Jesus' clothes. It is not business as usual; not just another day. Rather, like the women at the cross, let us stand by Jesus, look full in his face, and mourn his death.

And so it is finished. Jesus, the beloved Master, is dead. He has been tenderly and carefully anointed and placed in a borrowed grave. We breathe a sigh of relief. It is over; we can turn our thoughts from death to resurrection. But wait—not so fast. Easter will come soon enough. Like the disciples, may we carry the grief and pain of the cross with us until the dawn of Easter Day. May those who see our faces on this holiest of days see and understand the passion of our Lord. May we dwell—not morbidly, but gratefully and humbly—on what Christ has done for us. And may we understand anew how much God so loved the world. Amen.

SUGGESTIONS FOR WORSHIP

Opening Words and Prayer

LEADER: Let us pray to God, who loved the world so much that God's only Son came to give us life.

PEOPLE: **Grant, O Lord, through our worship this day, that familiar words may have new meaning and that the habit of worship may be cleansed of all stale formality and mere ceremonial observance. May our hearts fathom the depth of your love for us and the depth of the suffering you experienced on our behalf. Through Christ our Lord we pray. Amen.**

Litany (from Isaiah 53:1-7)

LEADER: Who has believed what we have heard? And to whom has the arm of the LORD been revealed?

PEOPLE: **For he grew up before us like a young plant. He had no form or majesty that we should look at him, nothing in his appearance that we should desire him.**

LEADER: We despised and rejected him, he became a man of suffering, one acquainted with infirmity.

PEOPLE: **He was one from whom we hid our faces; we despised him and held him of no account.**

LEADER: Surely he has borne our infirmities and carried our diseases; yet we accounted him stricken by God, and afflicted.

PEOPLE: **But he was wounded for our transgressions, crushed for our iniquities; upon him was the punishment that made us whole, and by his bruises we are healed.**

ALL:	**We, like sheep, have gone astray; we have all turned to our own way.**
LEADER:	And the Lord has laid on him the iniquity of us all.

Benediction

LEADER:	By your wounded hands,
PEOPLE:	**Teach us diligence and generosity.**
LEADER:	By your wounded feet,
PEOPLE:	**Teach us steadfastness and perseverance.**
LEADER:	By your wounded and insulted head,
PEOPLE:	**Teach us patience, clarity, and self-mastery.**
LEADER:	By your wounded heart,
PEOPLE:	**Teach us love, teach us love, teach us love,**
ALL:	**O Master and Savior. Amen.**

1. Gerard S. Sloyan, *John: Interpretation Bible Commentary* (Atlanta: John Knox Press, 1988), 200.

2. Arthur Gossip, "John" in *The Interpreter's Bible Commentary,* vol. 8, ed. George Buttrick (Nashville: Abingdon Press, 1952), 767.

Easter Day

Elizabeth A. Pugh

Isaiah 25:6-9: The people of God anticipate their promised day of deliverance.

Psalm 118:1-2, 14-24: The psalmist praises God who has "become my salvation."

1 Corinthians 15:1-11: Paul relates the tradition of the Resurrection so that his readers may come to believe.

John 20:1-18: The disciples find the empty tomb, and the risen Christ appears to Mary Magdalene.

REFLECTIONS

Of all the Resurrection narratives contained in all of the Gospels, this is my favorite, for it gives the preacher seeking to engage issues of new life, new hope, and even new gender roles for women much to ponder. The writer does an amazing thing, for as the passage comes to a close, a woman is given the role of evangelist, the one who spreads the good news. Mary Magdalene is commissioned to take the word to the others when Jesus says, "Go instead to my brothers and tell them, 'I am returning to my Father and your Father, to my God and your God'" (NIV).

The story begins in sadness and disbelief, and ends with unfathomable joy and the command, "Go and tell!" This pattern of life, where persons find themselves in the midst of tremendous loss only to suddenly and strangely realize that what they least expected to be a blessing has somehow come with surprise and power into their lives, is amazing. And when this sort of transformation, transition, migration of spirit happens to you, you can't help telling others about it.

This is what draws me. It is the real life *and* the ethereal within John's presentation. It is earthy and vivid, and at the same time mysterious and mystical, reminding the reader that when our pain is so fresh, our loss so all-encompassing, God's love and comfort show up, and we are stunned by its power. And we are so stunned that we must share it with others.

A SERMON BRIEF

Facing Today and Tomorrow

One day my mother called, somewhat disturbed by something that had happened to her earlier that day. She had been out doing some errands and had driven past my father's cemetery plot. A group of people was on the grass around the gravesite, and they were not people that she recognized immediately. Her heart filled with confusion and questions. What were they doing? Why were they at his grave? She decided to drive into the cemetery, and as she approached my father's grave, she began to recognize some of the people. They were youth from our church. Actually, the group had been talking about death and had come to my father's grave because he had recently died, and he was someone they knew.

My mother reported to me that she sat and talked with them, reminding them that she, too, would be buried in this place. As I talked with her about this intense and unexpected object lesson, I realized that this experience had touched a still raw place in her and had irritated this wound of suffering and loss.

Mary Magdalene also came to a place of burial, the tomb of Jesus, knowing the reality of his death, but now someone had intensified those feelings of loss for her by taking his body. Who were the two in the tomb? What was the gardener doing there? Did he take the body? I can see my mother's face. I can see Mary's face. Both, full of fear, concern, anxiety, confusion, and pain; eyes brimming with tears. The pain of loss still so tender, so near, so fresh, and a host of intruders just to complicate the situation further.

When we face such loss, we also come to understand that our emotions are complex and many. We feel sad and abandoned when a loved one dies. But we may also feel frustrated and angry with the person for leaving us. And no matter how mature and theologically astute we think we are, our first responses are always "Why?" and "Why me?"

I wish I could ask Mary what she felt. I wish I knew if she were angry with God for allowing this to happen, if she were angry with Jesus for not being more careful or not fighting back as he went to his death, or at least hiding from his enemies.

The story says that she stayed at the tomb after the disciples returned home. The reality of Jesus' death was still so real for her, so heavy, and the fact that someone had taken his body was just too much to handle. Who would do such a thing? She was lost in so much pain that in turning and looking at Jesus, she did not even know it was Jesus. How could she not know it was Jesus? It was her tremendous attachment to him that had caused her to remain at the tomb. But even face-to-face with her Lord, she did not know him. Her grief was inconsolable, for even Christ himself could not bring her comfort. The reality of his death was clear and final. She had seen it with her own eyes, and this memory would never be erased.

Mary is so much like us, for in the excruciating pain of loss, we can look Jesus right in the face and no peace comes; no calm is brought to our pained souls, no hope is believed. And this is sometimes the end of the story, or at least the place where we get stuck in our experience. But this is not God's experience. Our reality is different from God's reality. It is irony, for what we see as lost, as unredeemable, as hopeless, God takes hold of and renews. The appearance of our reality, which is genuine and real, is contrasted with God's reality, a plan for victory, not death. The human conflicts with the divine, belief with unbelief, and light with darkness.

What do we do with this claim, this reality that goes above and beyond our present pain and anguish, and yet at the same time enters our present reality? How do we proclaim something so incredible that all we can do is proclaim it? We cannot know for sure that beyond death something wonderful and spectacular awaits us, but still, we must surrender to the hope. For faith is somewhere between believing and knowing, trusting in God's love and still wanting assurances all along the way.

A dear chaplain friend told me a story while we were in seminary of a four-year-old little girl with leukemia. He had worked with this child for many months, and each time he came to see her, she requested that he read a particular story. It was her favorite. He would read it every time he came in, but she would always stop him right before the last page, never allowing him to read the final words of the story. One day he came in and they went through the ritual. And when they came to the next to the last page she did not reach up to close the book as she had done a million times before. She turned the page herself and allowed him to read the final words. Later that same day, she died.

This little one did not have words that would lead us to believe that she was a faithful Christian, facing death without fear. But at the same time, she must have believed that there was something okay about saying good-bye to this world so deliberately. She must have trusted or hoped that peace, rest, and painlessness were awaiting her. There must have been hope for tomorrow that let her release so willingly her grip on today.

For whatever reason, we have not been given the ability always to see the gates of heaven or the mysteries of God, but we do have Jesus who called out to Mary in her painful reality and touched her with God's reality. And most of all, we have an empty cross, which gives us peace today and hope for tomorrow.

SUGGESTIONS FOR WORSHIP

Call to Worship

LEADER: On this mountain the Lord of hosts will make for all peoples a feast of rich food,

PEOPLE: **And God will destroy on this mountain the shroud that is cast over all peoples, the sheet that is spread over all nations; God will swallow up death forever.**

LEADER: Then the Lord God will wipe away the tears from all faces, for the Lord has spoken.

PEOPLE: **It will be said on that day, Lo, this is our God; we have waited for God so that God might save us.**

LEADER: This is the Lord for whom we have waited; let us be glad and rejoice in God's salvation.

Benediction

And now go out into the world in peace, in the power and promise of the Resurrection. Go out not as those who weep with despair, but as those who, like Mary, have been touched and transformed by the presence of the risen Christ. Amen.

Second Sunday of Easter

Katherine Thomas Paisley

Acts 4:32-35: The community of believers is united in heart and soul, sees possessions as communal assets, testifies with power, and cares for one another.

Psalm 133: Unity among people is a blessing and sign of the presence of God.

1 John 1:1–2:2: The power of the Resurrection in the early Christian community means fellowship and a living witness of Christ's light.

John 20:19-31: The fearful disciples experience the risen Christ, and then Thomas does also, experiencing peace and a commissioning.

REFLECTIONS

In the first scene of the Gospel text, the disciples are gathered in fear and hidden in a locked room. Suddenly, the risen Jesus appears among them, saying, "Peace be with you." To a people bound by fear, there are no more welcome words. After repeating this blessing, Jesus gently reminds them of their task, "As the Father has sent me, so I send you," and breathes on them the Holy Spirit. The depth of their fear heightened the impact of the blessing of peace Jesus gave, and the Spirit's empowering enabled them to powerfully proclaim the message of the Resurrection! It is only after they receive both peace and the Spirit that they receive their new commission.

We don't know why Thomas wasn't there at the first appearance. Although we know him as "the Doubter," that isn't fair considering that with the disciples there was a whole lot of doubting going on. Thomas was the brave one in chapter 11. When the rest of the disciples want Jesus to avoid Bethany as a dangerous location, Thomas bravely suggests, "Let us also go, that we may die with him" (11:16*b*).

Jesus' second appearance may be especially for Thomas who, unafraid to die, may have been afraid to live without Jesus. Perhaps it is a measure of Thomas's faith that he doesn't dare believe the stories of the Resurrection without the proof of his own senses!

First John 1:1–2:2 complements the story of Thomas in suggesting the reality of the Resurrection as something the early Christian community saw and heard, and which had a claim upon their lives.

A SERMON BRIEF

What If I Do Believe?

Through the years, Thomas has gotten a bad rap. Unfairly so, perhaps. After all, when Mary Magdalene returned, having seen the risen Lord, all the disciples except Thomas gathered together behind a locked door, full of fear and trembling. They didn't throw a party or proclaim the story. They doubted, were afraid, and hid. Jesus appeared, showed them his hands and his side, repeated his message of peace for them, and breathed the Holy Spirit on them. Apparently, their fear and doubts were laid to rest because they told Thomas that they had seen the Lord.

Thomas's statement that he would need the evidence of his own senses doesn't seem unreasonable to us. After all, the story is far-fetched. Reasonable skepticism is a sign of intelligence! Truth verified objectively, in a lab or with scientific observation, is more easily believed. Of course we can relate to Thomas!

Crises of faith are not uncommon among us, when the world no longer makes sense and we cry out, "Where are you, God?"—times when we outgrow our childhood faith and must figure out for ourselves what is true. Perhaps Thomas wondered, "What am I going to do with the rest of my life now that my plans are in ruins at my feet?" We can respect that. Trusting in God would not allow a self-respecting finance committee to approve a building plan on a *Field of Dreams* faith—"If you build it, they will come." We can't just trust God for our future—we need a retirement plan. Fortunately for us, Jesus did not condemn Thomas for his doubt; he just reached out to him in his crisis and said, "Peace be with you."

Rediscovering faith requires another road for those of us who don't have the benefit of a physical appearance by the post-Easter Jesus. We need another way to make sense of life among the confusion or the ruins of faith. Marcus Borg, biblical scholar and member of the Jesus Seminar, discusses the post-Easter Jesus as real, living power in a different form from the living, historical Jesus. This power empowered the early Christians to live out their faith. The band of dynamic evangelists of the rest of Acts bears little resemblance to the fearful group behind a locked door in today's story.

To renew our faith we don't need to check our brains at the church door, nor do we need to somehow move beyond our doubt and "just believe in Jesus!" We do, however, need to open our minds to more possibilities than can be empirically proved. We need to be able to contemplate more truths than are found in human philosophy. Perhaps the greatest scientist of our generation declared, "There are only two ways to live your life. One is as though nothing is a miracle. The other is as though everything is a miracle." If Einstein could retain a sense of the miraculous, we too can contemplate the possibility of things beyond our understanding without giving up our intellectual integrity.

"Peace be with you" are wonderful words, but we need to remember their context. We aren't talking here about freedom from conflict or a life on easy street. This peace that Jesus gives is peace in the very thick of things—in the middle of trouble. It is the peace that Jesus had before Pilate, peace as a congregation gathers in loving embrace amid the ruins of a church torn by tornadoes. This peace enables us to go about our tasks even in the midst of conflict, even in a world that denies all that we believe, and, for the disciples, even under the threat of death.

Once we believe and receive the peace of Jesus, we have a task. Belief itself is not the objective. The post-Easter Jesus was concerned about the transmission of the message of justice and love even after he was out of the immediate picture. "As the Father has sent me, so I send you!" "To do the same things Jesus did?" we ask with dismay. "Yes," he replies, and the empowering breath of the Spirit is given. Talk about faith—God has entrusted the message of the gospel to a group of very unreliable witnesses—us!

The reality of Jesus among us gives us the vision and the courage to be his continued presence in the world! Faith, real faith, shatters our fear—but also destroys the peace that we know in the world! We desperately need Jesus' peace—because the other kind is forever gone! No more simply enjoying a movie—now we consider its message, and what nuances of selfishness and evil we must resist in our own thoughts. No more simple obedience at work without considering if the action will witness to the light that we serve. We can't just spend our money for whatever we want—we know that an account will be demanded of our stewardship. No longer will we simply blend in with the culture around us. Instead, we will be a light in the midst of

the general darkness. Faith demands not only a decision, but action—
a commitment to be about God's project to change the world.

A four-year-old girl was asked what God's love meant to her. She
said, "Knowing that God loves me is like walking in a rainbow—and
I have to share it, because it's not my rainbow." Thomas, longing for
a new vision, would have agreed.

SUGGESTIONS FOR WORSHIP

Call to Worship

LEADER: Lord, we gather as people who need something in
            which to believe.
PEOPLE: **We find it hard to believe in anything.**
LEADER: Help us find your presence, despite our fear and disbelief.
PEOPLE: **Come among us, Lord. Fill us with your Spirit and**
            your vision. Amen.

Prayer of Confession

Lord, we come filled with doubts, but afraid to speak them. We have
doubts about you and doubts about our place in the world. We don't
want to allow you into our lives completely. Often we give up trying to
make a difference because the task is overwhelming. Forgive us our fears.
Forgive our doubts. Open our eyes and minds to see your truth, wherever
it is found. Open our hearts to your loving purpose for the world. Fill us
with your Spirit to give us the courage to be your faithful people. Amen.

Benediction (from 1 John 1)

This is the message we have heard from him and proclaim to you,
that God is light and in him there is no darkness at all. Go as the light
of Christ in the world!

Music Suggestions

For contemporary worship: Michael W. Smith and Brent Bourgeois,
"Live the Life," or "Redeemer," by Nicole Coleman-Mullen
For children: "Take All of Me" by Tommy, Tyler, and Eric Coomes

Third Sunday of Easter

Elizabeth Bridges Ford

Acts 3:12-19: Peter preaches Jesus Christ to the Israelites gathered in Solomon's Portico.

Psalm 4: The psalmist cries out to God for answers and comes to a renewed knowledge of the presence and care of God.

1 John 3:1-7: John reminds believers that they are children of God and admonishes them to seek purity and reject sin.

Luke 24:36b-48: Jesus appears among the gathered disciples who are following to confirm the truth of his resurrection, and commissions them as his witnesses.

REFLECTIONS

Seeing is believing, or so the saying goes; yet how often our eyes play tricks on us! We need only think of M. C. Escher's confounding images to remember. In some of Escher's drawings, perspective shifts in such a way that the foreground and the background each produce their own subjects. Is this an image of fish or birds?[1] Are the stairs ascending or descending?[2] It is no wonder the disciples didn't trust their eyes on that Easter evening.

Still, it is striking how intentionally Jesus gives the disciples tangible proof that it is he. "Look at my hands and my feet; see that it is I myself." Although he invites them to "touch and see," no one accepts Jesus' invitation to touch. The focus remains on seeing. What is it about seeing that is so essential to the Christian faith?

Part of our task as people of faith is to learn to attune ourselves to recognize the ways in which God is at work in our lives, to detect signs of God's presence. The risen Christ presents himself to the disciples in the midst of their "disbelieving and wondering," and he comes to us as well.

At times, physical sight may be a barrier because it doesn't lead to the more profound insights that we can only perceive internally. Jesus takes the disciples to this deeper level by opening the Scriptures to them, as God's Word illumines our understanding.

Jesus opens their hearts and minds to see who he is so that they might believe and trust in him and, through their witness, lead others to believe. Thus, I wonder if it is more apt to say that "believing is seeing," for belief leads to new kinds of sight. Believing transforms the way we see the world around us.

A SERMON BRIEF

Believing Is Seeing

Their day began with a jolt. Just after dawn, the women burst in. "He wasn't there, he is risen!" Their excitement sent the disciples reeling. They just couldn't take it in. It was hard enough to believe that he was gone. How could they believe that he was here again? And later in the day, the two returned from Emmaus. "We saw him. We recognized him when he broke the bread and gave it to us. How our hearts burned within us as he spoke!" They were still talking about it when Jesus slipped in, saying, "Peace be with you."

How different the Resurrection appearances are from the stories of Jesus' birth! This time, there is no heavenly host pointing the way to Jesus. No angels sing, "Glory to God in the highest." There are no shepherds, no wise men, no star. The people don't go looking for Jesus, but he comes to them. He comes and stands among them in the midst of their darkness and doubt, their grief and confusion, and he still does.

In her book *Traveling Mercies,* Anne Lamott describes a time when Jesus came to her. Steeped in the drug culture of the 1960s, Lamott chronicles her spiritual journey in language that is raw and real. In one scene, she has just had an abortion. Very drunk, she lies down, shaky and scared. "After a while, as I lay there, I became aware of someone with me, hunkered down in the corner.... The feeling was so strong that I actually turned on the light for a moment to make sure no one was there—of course, there wasn't. But after a while, in the dark again, I knew beyond any doubt that it was Jesus. I felt him just sitting there on his haunches in the corner of my sleeping loft, watching me with patience and love, and I squinched my eyes shut, but that didn't help because that's not what I was seeing him with."[3] Jesus stays with her.

Jesus comes to us in the midst of real life, when we most need him.

He comes to the disciples in the midst of their grief, and to a woman who is feeling alone and afraid. He meets us where we are and gives us what we need to believe. John Calvin calls this God's "accommodation" to humanity. The Holy One bows before us, bending to our level. As a nurse coos to an infant, Calvin says God "lisps" to us, speaking to us in baby talk.[4] God gives us what we need to recognize that we are not alone and to grasp the holy mystery that is beyond our comprehension.

Isn't this the essence of the incarnation, God's self-revelation in Jesus Christ? Jesus reveals himself to the disciples by showing them his hands and feet. "See, I am not a ghost. It is I, myself." Could it be? *How* could it be? Our text says the disciples were "disbelieving for joy."

Sometimes life is so much better than we could ever imagine, that it almost doesn't compute. When my cousin learned that she was pregnant with triplets, she seemed "disbelieving for joy." Hearing the three heartbeats, seeing the sonogram—none of that was enough to make it sink in. Even after the babies were born, it didn't seem real. After years of longing, it was simply too good to be true.

So what exactly does it mean to believe? Is it a matter of resolving all of the questions we carry around in our heads? It seems to me that believing is more than mental gymnastics, more than verifying facts. It is more than mere "intellectual assent," as Kathleen Norris notes. In Greek, "to believe" means "to give one's heart to."[5] Believing encompasses more than our minds. It relates to where we place our trust. It is centered on the One in whom we place our trust.

What have you given your heart to? This is one of the questions that our confirmation class is pondering as they prepare to join the church. As they reflect on the questions that the session will ask them to affirm, we encourage them to consider the "therefore." "Trusting in the gracious mercy of God, I turn from the ways of sin and renounce evil and its power in the world; *therefore, . . .*" "I turn to Jesus Christ and accept him as my Lord and Savior, trusting in his grace and love; *therefore, . . .*" The "therefore" is the most important piece. It shows what difference these promises make in our lives.

Seeing Jesus' hands and feet and watching him eat broiled fish aren't in themselves enough to make the disciples believe. It isn't until Jesus turns their attention to the Scriptures that they truly see. He points them back to what they already know. He recalls the words he spoke to them while he was still with them, opening their minds to understand the Scriptures. How many times had they heard him say that he would suffer and die and on the third day be raised from the dead? Yet, now they see.

Believing is seeing. After we have given our hearts to Christ, we get new eyes with which to see and a new opportunity to encounter the risen Christ who comes to us again and again in the breaking of bread and in the midst of the Easter-storied community.

Believing is not only looking back and remembering. It is also looking forward. Our job is not only to be witnesses, but also to bear witness so that others might also see; to bear witness to the good news that we can turn to God and claim the forgiveness that God extends to us; to bear witness to the love of God that is present to us in the risen Christ; to bear witness to the good news that this love meets us where we are, in joy and in sorrow, in confusion and in clarity. Christ is risen. He brings us his peace, if we will only believe and see.

SUGGESTIONS FOR WORSHIP

Call to Worship (based on 1 John 3:1)

LEADER: See what love God has given us, that we should be called children of God. The peace of Christ be with you.

PEOPLE: **And also with you.**

Prayer of Confession

God of light, you know the sin that shrouds our hearts in darkness. We confess that we have not lived as witnesses to your love. Day by day, we close our eyes to the needs of those around us. We forget to love and serve you. We fail to seek your face. Have mercy on us, O God. Receive us, as you receive our prayer, for we put our trust in you.

Assurance of Pardon (based on Psalm 4)

The LORD hears your call.
May the gladness of God's grace be in your hearts.
May you rest in the shelter of God's forgiveness and love.

Benediction (based on Acts 3:15)

To this we are witnesses:
the God of life has come to us

in Jesus Christ, the risen One.
Go in peace,
believing that God goes before you,
that Christ stands beside you,
and that the Holy Spirit lives within you.

1. M. C. Escher, *Metamorphose II,* Woodcut, 1938–40.
2. M. C. Escher, *Ascending and Descending,* Lithograph, 1960.
3. Anne Lamott, *Traveling Mercies: Some Thoughts on Faith* (New York: Anchor Books, 1999), 49-50.
4. John Calvin, *Institutes of the Christian Religion,* I.13.1 (Philadelphia: Westminster Press, 1960), 121.
5. Kathleen Norris, *Amazing Grace: A Vocabulary of Faith* (New York: Riverhead Books, 1998), 62.

Fourth Sunday of Easter

Donna Hopkins Britt

Acts 4:5-12: Peter and John are brought before the Council in Jerusalem to defend their proclamation of Jesus Christ.

Psalm 23: The Lord is our shepherd, the one who tenderly cares for all our needs.

1 John 3:16-24: We know God's love through the sacrifice of Christ and the abiding presence of the Spirit.

John 10:11-18: Jesus is the Good Shepherd, the one who lays down his life for his sheep.

REFLECTIONS

Halfway through the season of Easter each year, we find "Good Shepherd Sunday." Gail O'Day cautions the homilist that Jesus as the Good Shepherd is a christological image, not one that we should transfer to pastor as shepherd.[1] All of us are the sheep; clergy and laity alike are to know and follow the Good Shepherd who selflessly lays down his life for his sheep.

The image tells of One of comfort, care, and guidance; One who will not leave us when we are in danger; and, from the psalm, One who refreshes and strengthens and blesses us. Jesus is also One who knows us, even when we may be reticent about sharing who we are with others. Jesus knows us, cares for us, and continues to call us to follow him, despite our resistance.

The simple message of the Gospel text (and there are many messages, such as unity, intimacy, sacrifice) is the reminder that the Good Shepherd cares for us deeply. That affects our lives. How, then, can we live gratefully?

A SERMON BRIEF

Following the Good Shepherd

"Sheep are dumb." At least that's what we've been told. But, according to at least one person who grew up on a sheep farm, sheep are not dumb. In this person's opinion, that we think sheep are dumb is the result of a false advertising ploy of cattle farmers. Cattle farmers move their herd from the back with horses and whips. Sheep, on the other hand, are led from the front, following their shepherd.[2] Different, but not dumb.

Not only that, sheep *know* their shepherd. In a *National Geographic* article from several years ago, the writer tells about the Rabari people in India, who are sheepherders. At night, shepherds and flocks gather in one place, and the shepherds take turns sharing night watchman duty.

The morning, then, is time for withdrawal to each flock's pasture. "Each shepherd has slightly different calls, variations on a theme. There are morning calls to move out, a call to bring the sheep to water, and so on. Each man knows his own sheep and vice versa, and his particular flock will disentangle itself from the larger flock and move out behind him in the morning."[3] This may or may not seem astonishing, until one realizes that perhaps five thousand sheep are gathered together in the single large nighttime flock.

Although many voices may be calling, sheep will follow only *their* shepherd. Sheep know their shepherd. Jesus said, "I know my own and my own know me" (John 10:14). "The LORD is my shepherd."

And shepherds know their sheep. For the shepherd, each sheep is a "who" and not a "what." The shepherd "is so intimately familiar with his own sheep that he will know at once who is present and who may yet be missing. And this despite the presence of perhaps thousands of other milling sheep—all looking, at least to the uninitiated—very much alike indeed."[4]

In the Gospel text, Jesus says, "I am the good shepherd." Jesus is not the "hired hand" who will run away at the first sign of danger. Instead, he cares for the sheep. "I know my own and my own know me," he says. Jesus is describing a relationship, an intimate relationship in which each partner knows the other deeply. As a child who has gotten away from his mother in a crowd will be comforted by hearing the sound of her voice, we know and desire to hear the voice of our Shepherd. As we can feel completely at ease with our best friends, so we can feel protected by the Good Shepherd. He is One who will search for us when we are lost, if only we are attentive to his call. "The L ORD is my shepherd, I shall not want."

One difference between us and true sheep, though, is that sheep don't seem to have a problem following their shepherd. If we know our Shepherd, and know that our Shepherd wants only what is good for our well-being, wants to care for us, wants to protect us, why do we wander off? Why do we try to escape his protective eyes and his voice that calls us to remain with his flock? Perhaps this could be termed SADD: Sheep Attention Deficit Disorder. We are so easily distracted by louder voices and enticing activities that summon our attention away from the call of the Shepherd.

We've heard that breakfast is the most important meal of the day. Most people who ignore breakfast tire more quickly and don't think as well, so the whole day suffers from not taking time for the body's nourishment.

The same is true for our spirits when we block out the voice of the Shepherd and do not accept the spiritual nourishment he offers. We might be more irritable. Decisions slam us in the face and we don't have as strong a sense of divine wisdom to choose well. A colleague or friend is in need of a listening ear, and we are too self-involved to notice; we are too distracted to notice.

But we have a Shepherd who would give up his life for his sheep. Not that that would be the best thing for the flock, but he loves his sheep so much that he would take the wolf's fangs for them. Our Shepherd is the One who does not turn away from watching over us. Our Shepherd is the One who will not be distracted by a plane zooming overhead or a cell phone call or the many tasks of the day. No, he's always vigilant, always listening, and always calling us back to the flock when we stray.

The selflessness of the Shepherd is a model for us. We have many claims on our time: family, friends, jobs, volunteer work, housework, and our own need for space. Sometimes the voices that call are those of the "hired hand," calls of those who do not care for the sheep as the Shepherd does. Sometimes these people or tasks sap our energy and then go away, and no one is the better for it.

The model of the Shepherd is constant care, and following him means we are responsible for being attentive to others' needs as well as our own. We need to keep our own "pitchers" full if we are to pour out energy for others.

The voice of the Shepherd is quiet, but urgent. "Listen to me, and follow," it says. It takes a decision early in the day to remind us to listen through the rest of the day. And every day it takes a new decision to choose to listen. The Gospel writer reminds us to listen and follow, listen and follow, listen and follow. "The LORD is my shepherd . . . and I shall dwell in the house of the LORD forever" (NIV).

SUGGESTIONS FOR WORSHIP

Call to Worship

LEADER: Good Shepherd, you have gathered us into your flock.
PEOPLE: **With thankful hearts we recognize you as our caretaker and our guide.**
LEADER: Call us to your nourishing pastures and quiet waters.
PEOPLE: **Restore our souls again, we ask, as we offer our lives to you.**

Prayer of Confession

Loving and generous God, with humility we bow our heads before your holiness. With contrite hearts, we become aware again of how generously you care for us and how you call us to care for one another. Forgive us, we pray, for ignoring you and ignoring our need for you. Forgive us for ignoring the needs of others. Forgive us for our selfishness.

Grant us strength and courage, we pray, to live as your faithful followers, caring for all in your world with the love and care you have shown to each of us.

Assurance of Pardon

God does not wish that we continue to sin. Having confessed our sins to our Lord, now let us remember and rejoice that Jesus Christ is risen and connects us once again with our holy God through gracious forgiveness. In the name of Jesus, we are forgiven.

Benediction

Go from this place, remembering that the Good Shepherd is with you, nourishing you and giving you guidance for each day.

1. Gail O'Day, "John" in *The New Interpreter's Bible* (Nashville: Abingdon Press, 1995), 672.

2. Barbara Brown Taylor, "The Voice of the Shepherd," *Pulpit Resource* 29, no. 2, year C (2001): 30.

3. Robyn Davidson, "Wandering with India's Rabari," *National Geographic* 184 (September 1993): 78.

4. Judy Buck-Glenn, "Serving the Word," *Homily Service* 34, no. 2 (May 6, 2001): 16.

Fifth Sunday of Easter

Florence E. Canada

Acts 8:26-40: The Ethiopian eunuch responds to the words of Scripture and the teaching of Philip, and asks to be baptized.

Psalm 22:25-31: The psalmist proclaims the eternal rule of God.

1 John 4:7-21: Because God first loved us in Jesus Christ, we are commanded to love others and abide in God's love.

John 15:1-8: Jesus is the true vine and we are the branches, those who are able to bear fruit because we are joined to him.

REFLECTIONS

By now, the fifth Sunday of Easter, we have journeyed through Lent and celebrated Easter Sunday. We have focused on the events leading up to the cross and have looked anew at Jesus' death and resurrection. Now we find ourselves in a season where our thoughts have turned to life on the other side of the cross. Therefore, it is a season most fitting for reflection on the expectation that we, as Jesus' disciples, are to bear fruit.

I want to look at this expectation by focusing on the promise, the hope, and the challenge of bearing fruit. Crucial to the manifestation of this expectation is the urging of Jesus to abide in him. The thought of bearing fruit by abiding in Jesus relieves anxiety and brings a sense of peace into our lives. Think about it: in a world where many people are constantly looking for new strategies for guaranteed success, Jesus assures us that all we have to do is abide in him.

May 18, 2003

A SERMON BRIEF

Abide in Him

I grew up on a farm. We planted several different kinds of crops on the farm, and each plant bore fruit according to its type. The tomato plants produced tomatoes, and the apple trees produced apples. Sometimes it was necessary to thin plants out when they got too thick, and to trim them if they started to grow in a way that was unnatural or unproductive. This used to upset me at first. However, my daddy explained that if corrective action were not taken, the entire plant would die. As time went by, I realized Daddy was right. Once pruned, the plants would grow and produce even more fruit.

Thoughts of my childhood on the farm came back to me as I reflected on the message Jesus shared with his disciples on the night he was betrayed. It is a message of promise, hope, and challenge. Jesus knew what waited just ahead for himself and for those who followed him. However, he told the disciples that as long as they abided in him, they had nothing to fear. As long as they abided in him, they would bear much fruit.

As Jesus spoke with his disciples that evening, he used an image the disciples were familiar with: the image of a vineyard. He took that which was familiar and gave it new meaning. In Jesus' example, God is the one who takes care of the garden. Jesus is the vine, and the disciples are the branches. Just as the tomato plants on the farm were always expected to bear tomatoes, the disciples were expected to bear the same fruit as the vine to which they were attached. They were to continue the work Jesus had started—the work of saving, healing, delivering, and setting free those who were trapped in illness and sin; the work of teaching, preaching, and living the gospel; the work of praising God, worshiping God, and giving God the glory through their lives. That is the fruit: fruit that is manifested in lives transformed and improved by the power of the Holy Spirit.

As Jesus taught the disciples, when it comes to bearing fruit, there are four possible scenarios. The first possibility is that the branch will not bear any fruit. The second possibility is that the branch will bear *some* fruit. The third possibility is that the branch will bear more fruit. And last, it is possible that the branch will bear *much* fruit. But Jesus assures his disciples that if they are diligent about abiding in him, they will be those who bear much fruit. This is the promise. The promise assures them that they do not have to try to *make* things happen; they

111

do not have to depend on their own intellect, talent, or ability. All they have to do is abide in Jesus. They must live the way he taught them to live during his three years with them. They must hold on to his teachings by believing them in their hearts and allowing them to be the guiding rubrics for their lives and ministries. Most important of all, they must walk in love. This is the evidence or mark of abiding in him. If they abide in him, Jesus promises that they will bear much fruit. God will be glorified, and many lives will be transformed.

Jesus also tells his disciples that as they begin to bear fruit, God will help them bear even more fruit through the process of pruning. This is what my daddy was doing when he would clip and trim some of the plants on the farm. When the gardener prunes a plant, he clips away the things that are preventing their growth. When God prunes, God also clips away those attitudes, habits, thoughts, and unhealthy attachments to things and people that get in the way of bearing fruit.

Of course, pruning can be painful. I know from personal experience. However, once all the stuff that is dangerous and detrimental to us is gone, we are much more healthy and productive. We bear more fruit. Herein lies the hope: the hope that no matter where we are now in our walk with God, God will not give up on us. God will continue to lovingly care for us, mold us, shape us, and prune us until we move to a place where we are bearing fruit. As we abide in Jesus, we will move to the point where Jesus is not just our Savior and our Lord, but our friend as well. We will move to the point where we can be completely honest with him, cry with him, laugh with him, and be silent with him.

There is promise, and there is hope. But there is also challenge. The challenge is to be faithful, to be committed to the same priorities Jesus had. We must desire to bear the same kind of fruit he bore and never forget that abiding in him is the key to our productivity. As we spend time with Jesus, the power and presence of the Holy Spirit will more fully rest upon us. But if we turn from him, we will begin to wither and die. Apart from Jesus, we can do nothing, but with him all things are possible.

As we abide in him, we experience his love, and as we experience his love, we learn more fully how to love God and one another. You can't help it because Jesus is the full expression of God, and God is love. We can volunteer for every project, teach Sunday school, and give a lot of money for good causes. We can do all this and more— but if we do not have love, God is still not glorified. As we spend time with Jesus, as we abide in him, he will teach us how to love.

Jesus has extended the promise, and if we grasp that promise, it will give us hope. However, the challenge is whether or not we are willing to do our part. It is a question of whether or not we are willing to trust God enough to place the people and the things we love the most into God's hands. But there is also an invitation here: an invitation to get to know Jesus better. As we spend time with Jesus, we, like the disciples who gathered with him on the night he was betrayed, can move to the point where Jesus is not only our Savior and our Lord, but he is also our friend. Accept the promise, the hope, and the challenge. Abide in him.

SUGGESTIONS FOR WORSHIP

Call to Worship

LEADER: Dear friends, let us love one another.
PEOPLE: **For God is love.**
LEADER: Dear friends, let us share our love with others.
PEOPLE: **For God is love.**

Prayer of Confession

Gracious God, we confess that often we have not walked in your love. Too often we have failed to love one another; too often we have failed to share our love with those outside this community of faith. Gracious God, help us more fully understand and walk in your love. Help us be your instruments of salvation, healing, deliverance; help us live in such a way that you are glorified. [A time of silent prayer.]

Assurance of Pardon

As we cry out to God in our sin, God is faithful to forgive us and to cleanse us. Enter in and receive your cleansing. Rise up and walk anew in the light of God's love.

Benediction

As we depart, let us go forward with the peace and joy of God's love in our hearts. Let us go into the world to bear much fruit. Amen.

Sixth Sunday of Easter

Felecia T. Douglass

Acts 10:44-48: The Holy Spirit falls upon the Gentiles.

Psalm 98: Creation sings God's praise.

1 John 1:5-6: Those who love God obey God.

John 15:9-17: Jesus calls his disciples not servants, but friends.

REFLECTIONS

Before Jesus' crucifixion, he gathered his disciples to instruct them. Here Jesus radically redefines his relationship with his disciples, calling them not servants, but friends. Next he defines that friendship: one of *his* choosing, one of full disclosure and reciprocity, and one where disciples are commanded to love as he loved them. It's that last phrase that is the problem, for as long as friendship with Jesus is not defined by self-sacrificial love, it is achievable. People only want to make sacrifices that have certain outcomes, which, of course, aren't sacrifices at all.

In this sermon, I decided to be honest about my fear of making sacrifices. I tell a series of stories about smaller sacrifices, those I am more comfortable making. Each story builds toward the final sacrifice—laying down one's life for one's friend. Here I tell the story of Father Maximillian Kolbe, who died in another prisoner's place at Auschwitz. That story naturally leads to Jesus' own sacrifice.

I include a wordplay on the word thanks *(eucharisto)*, since this sermon concludes with the Lord's Supper. This sermon was first preached in chapel at Central Baptist Theological Seminary in Kansas City.

A SERMON BRIEF
Just What You Do

I don't know about you, but when I read about Jesus' dying on our behalf, I get a little tense. It's not that I don't believe the Bible. On the contrary, I believe so much that I fear someone will ask me to make a similar sacrifice—but not that I will lay down my life; not anything that big. Sometimes I don't even like the day-to-day sacrifices. I'm not making excuses, but my life has been difficult and I want to hold on to what I have and never let go. Sacrifice when you don't have much to begin with? No way.

Besides, I often ask, "Is there anything worth the sacrifice?" I don't mean to be insulting, but my loved ones are really pretty normal, somewhat flawed. If I'm going to sacrifice on their behalf, I want them to be worth it!

I want small risk and big dividends. I want a guaranteed outcome. In my search for an answer I've met some interesting people. Meet Jennifer. She's our favorite baby-sitter. Picture this event in her life: she and her family are seated around the kitchen table. In front of them are little slips of paper. They are about to vote for a much-needed family vacation. Mother was laid off when the factory closed and they have scrimped for two years for a dream vacation. It's a tie. Dad and Steven vote for the beach, and Mom and Jennifer for the mountains. You can tell by the looks on their faces that neither side will compromise. Can you blame them? These are their dreams. Steven, angry and disappointed, runs to his room and slams the door. He begins to cry.

Jennifer listens outside Steven's door before going to bed. The next morning she swings her vote for the beach. Is this a case of "greater love hath no one . . . "? When I asked Jennifer why she sacrificed her vacation, she shrugged her shoulders, "It's just what you do when you're in a family." Well, maybe.

Her brother keeps a memento from that trip—a picture of the sunset at Edisto Island. He uses that picture as a marker to remind him to say thanks.

Meet Joe. He's a hard-working, thirty-five-year-old father of four. Joe and Sally recently took their kids clothes shopping. Their kids have grown out of everything. That night, after the bedtime stories, Sally looked at Joe and laughed. His faded blue jeans had sprouted a hole in one knee. Who knew when *those* jeans could be replaced? Joe touched the hole and shrugged his shoulders, "It's just what you do when you're a parent." Well, maybe.

Joe and Sally's kids grew up. Whenever they see a picture of their dad, they laugh at his old blue jeans with the hole. Seeing those jeans reminds them to say thanks to parents who gave up much to keep them clothed.

Meet Mark. He and Sarah had been married almost twenty years when Sarah decided to go to seminary and become a hospital chaplain. Only there was one small problem—the seminary was in another state. Since Mark could practice his profession anywhere, they moved to pursue her dream. Is this a case of "greater love hath no one . . . "? When I commended Mark on his sacrifice, he shrugged his shoulders, "I guess it's just what you do when you're married." Well, maybe.

Every morning, when Sarah puts on her clerical collar, she remembers to say thanks to the one who gave up part of his life for her dream.

Meet Stephanie. She had her world shattered when her daughter Rachel was killed in an automobile accident. As if the shock of her loss were not enough, Stephanie found out that Rachel had filled out an organ donation card. The doctors wanted to harvest her organs. Stephanie agonized over her decision, while the doctors kept the body alive. Organ donation just made her death so final. She wanted to remember Rachel the way she was. When asked later why she fulfilled Rachel's wishes, she replied with a grief-laden shrug, "It gave Rachel's loss some meaning."

Somewhere a man named Bryan considers each sight through new corneas a marker reminding him to say thanks. A man named Henry now has a strong heart, and whenever he wrestles with his grandchildren, he remembers to say thanks to Rachel, whose death gave him life.

Meet Maximillian Kolbe. He was a Franciscan priest who had sheltered Jews and was condemned to Auschwitz in 1941. In July of that year, there was an escape. It was customary to kill ten prisoners for every one who escaped. The Nazis denied the ten food and water until they died in agony.

The commandant lined the prisoners up and randomly called names. As one of the prisoners stumbled forward to fulfill this monstrous quota, he wept out these words, "My wife, my children." His name was Gajowniczek. As he was escorted away, the officers heard movement among the prisoners. The guards raised their rifles. A prisoner was leaving the lineup and pushing his way to the front.

It was Father Kolbe, no fear on his face, no hesitancy in his step. "I wish to speak to the commandant. I wish to take this prisoner's place." He pointed to Gajowniczek. "I have no wife, no children, besides I am old and no longer good for anything." "Request granted."

Gajowniczek writes later, "Prisoners were never allowed to speak . . . I could only thank him with my eyes." Father Kolbe outlived the other nine. He had to be killed by lethal injection. It was August 14th, 1941. Is this a case of "greater love hath no one . . . "?

Gajowniczek survived the Holocaust and was reunited with his family. Every year he returns to Auschwitz to remember Father Kolbe. In his backyard sits a plaque carved by his own hand. It stands as a marker so he will always remember to say thank you to the man who died in his place.[1]

Meet one more Jew. One of many who have died over the years as a result of martyrdom, persecution, and pogroms. His story is not too different from the others. And if you could ask him about his sacrifice, maybe he would shrug his shoulders ever so slightly while he looked you right in the eye and said, "It's just what you do when you love people so much you'd do anything to save them." That's a paraphrase of "No one has greater love than this, to lay down one's life for one's friends."

My sisters and brothers, it was some two thousand years ago that Jesus looked at us and called us friends. What kind of marker would you use to remind you to say thank you to the one who sacrificed his life for you?

You know, we have such a marker. We call it the Lord's Supper. In Greek it is called *eucharisto*, which means thanksgiving. Will you do me a favor? While you partake of the bread and wine, will you remember to say thanks?

SUGGESTIONS FOR WORSHIP

Call to Worship (based on Psalm 98)

LEADER: Make a joyful noise to the Lord, all the earth; break forth into joyous song and sing praises.

PEOPLE: Sing praises to the Lord with the lyre, with the lyre and the sound of melody.

LEADER: Let the sea roar and all that fills it, the world and those who live in it.

PEOPLE: Let the floods clap their hands; let the hills sing together for the joy at the presence of the Lord,

LEADER: For God is coming to judge the earth.

PEOPLE: God will judge the world with righteousness, and the peoples with equity.

1. This story can be found in Max Lucado, *Six Hours One Friday: Anchoring to the Power of the Cross* (Portland, Oreg.: Multnomah Publishers, 1989), as well as in Patricia Treece, *A Man for Others* (San Francisco: Harper & Row, 1982).

Ascension of the Lord

Marjorie A. Menaul

Acts 1:1-11: The report of the promise of the gift of the Holy Spirit and the ascension of Jesus into heaven.

Psalm 47: A psalm praising God's rule over all people and nations.

Ephesians 1:15-23: The writer to the Ephesians prays for wisdom for those who testify to the glory of Christ.

Luke 24:44-53: Jesus commissions the disciples to bear witness to his life, death, and resurrection and then ascends into heaven in their presence.

REFLECTIONS

In liturgical churches, the season of Advent is a time of preparation for the twelve-day celebration of the Incarnation. During the season of Lent, Christians are called to prepare for the celebration of the Resurrection, which lasts for fifty days. But the third chief festival of the Christian year, the celebration of the gift of the Holy Spirit at Pentecost, comes and goes very quickly. Preparation for Pentecost can get lost in the celebration of Easter. Once the day of Pentecost has come and gone, the long green season of summer closes in quickly.

It can be tempting for the preacher to skip directly from Easter to Pentecost, without dealing with the part of the story that Luke/Acts places between them. Luke's two volumes may present the Ascension story differently (locating it on different days, with different details), but they have this in common: they tell of Jesus' promise to his friends that they will receive power from on high, and show him departing from them with only the promise to cling to.

Jesus has ascended to glory with God; that is one side of the story. But from the disciples' side, Ascension meant that Jesus was no longer a part of their daily life. The Holy Spirit had not yet been given. We

118

should indeed celebrate the glory of Christ, risen and ascended. But there is also a human reality to be recognized here, an awkward gap in the story. Our lives are so often full of awkward gaps! And Luke thought this one was worth talking about. The sermon that follows is one way to begin that conversation.

A SERMON BRIEF

An evening at the theater can be one of life's delights. Getting dressed up; meeting friends; being led into another world, populated by real human beings—there is a lot to recommend it. In the midst of all the positives, however, there is one element I would really rather do without: intermission. When we've become immersed in a compelling story, when we've learned to care about some, if not all, of the characters, it's a jolt to see the curtain come down, the lights go up, and everyone start to stretch and talk and head for the bathroom. The dramatic world has vanished, and mundane life is back with a vengeance.

Intermission always comes just when you've truly moved inside the story. You began on the outside looking in, but as you've come to know the characters and the relationships, you've lost sight of your own separateness and become part of what's happening. And it never fails—just when you're really involved, you're cut off. Left hanging. Compelling drama gives way to social chitchat and lines at the ladies' room.

Sure, the actors need a pause; I understand that. Sure, the audience needs a drink of water and a chance to stretch their legs. Some playgoers may even take advantage of the intermission to talk about the play—to help one another notice bits and pieces they'd missed, and perhaps speculate about where the playwright means to go. There is plenty to do, but it's all beside the point. It's like putting a coffee hour in the middle of a worship service, or dessert in the middle of dinner. If you've been counting on something of real substance, even though intermission is generally pleasant enough, it feels more and more like empty time.

Then, finally the lights flash. People begin politely climbing over one another to return to their seats. The curtain rises. And the drama reaches out to engage us once again.

In the Gospel of Luke and the book of Acts, Luke draws his readers into the two-act drama of salvation as a playwright might draw an audience into a play. In each volume, the curtain falls on Jesus' earthly life as the resurrected Jesus leaves his disciples and is carried up out of their sight. Until now, Jesus has been the chief actor in the drama. From his birth to his death to his resurrection appearances, it is Jesus who has kept the story moving. And now he's gone—offstage once and for all.

The curtain has fallen.

Is the drama over? By no means! It's simply intermission.

Christians tend to be as uncomfortable with this intermission in the salvation story as I am with intermissions at the theater. Caught up in events of Jesus' death and resurrection, we're ready to rush right along into the second act—to skip ahead to the gift of the Holy Spirit and what it made possible. If we didn't, we'd have to deal with a very troubling question. Without Jesus' presence among them any longer, without the Holy Spirit to energize them yet, were the disciples simply adrift during the ten days between the Ascension and Pentecost? Was it just empty time?

Luke doesn't seem to think so. From the book of Acts: "[Jesus] ordered them not to leave Jerusalem, but to wait there for the promise of the Father. 'This,' he said, 'is what you have heard from me; for John baptized with water, but you will be baptized with the Holy Spirit not many days from now.' "

From the Gospel: "See, I am sending upon you what my Father promised; so stay here in the city until you have been clothed with power from on high." And then, after Jesus had left them, Luke says, "They worshiped him, and returned to Jerusalem with great joy; and they were continually in the temple blessing God."

Jesus had left them, and the disciples waited. It must have been hard for them, as it is for us—waiting is nobody's favorite occupation. Standing in a line that doesn't move; watching the clock in a crowded doctor's office; checking each day's mail in the hope that the check will finally come—when the wait really matters, it's hard to feel anything but impatience and frustration. Why can't we just get on with it?

We're impatient. Like the disciples, we're likely to turn our impatience, not only toward other people, but toward God as well.

- If Jesus came to fulfill God's plan of salvation, why didn't he carry it right through to the end, all at once? The disciples' question was a good one—why not "restore the kingdom to Israel"?
- If the problem with that question was that Jesus wanted his kingdom to include more than Israel, why didn't he send the Holy

Spirit right then, and get the disciples moving immediately to spread the good news?

• The Holy Spirit was poured out on the church a long time ago. Why are we *still* waiting for the fulfillment of the promises of God?

Why wait? I don't know the answers to those questions. Only God does. As Jesus told his friends, long ago, "It is not for you to know the times or periods that the Father has set by his own authority. But you will receive power when the Holy Spirit has come upon you; and you will be my witnesses" (Acts 1:7-8).

If the time *we're* living in seems like an intermission in the carrying out of God's plan of salvation, then we need to wait for God. If the time *you're* living in seems like an intermission in God's plan for your life—if Jesus has vanished from your sight, and the Holy Spirit's power is only a distant promise—then it's your job to wait. Not just to kill time, but to wait as the disciples waited; with trust and hope; with eagerness for the beginning of the next act.

We could make other choices, of course. You and I can fill our time with social chitchat and refreshments, until intermission-filling activities become the most important thing in our lives. We can even leave the theater altogether, and go off to find another story to give meaning to our lives.

But there is no other story that will do. It is God who gives meaning to our lives, and gives it in God's own time. In recognition of that reality, let us live through our intermissions as the disciples lived through theirs.

When nothing much seemed to be happening, and they couldn't see where the future would lead them, during the intermission, they remained focused on the drama of salvation, and worshiped God with great joy. Their joyful worship as they waited helped them center themselves in the promises of God.

Much as we delight in getting things done, God's promises are more reliable than our accomplishments. Like the disciples, we have the promises of God to cling to. Those promises are ours, even at times when it seems that Christ has vanished and the Holy Spirit is not breathing down our necks or in our lives.

Cling to the promises. Rejoice in them. And be ready for the curtain to go up. Because in God, there surely will be a second act.

SUGGESTIONS FOR WORSHIP

Call to Worship (from Psalm 47)

LEADER: Clap your hands, all you peoples; shout to God with loud songs of joy.

PEOPLE: **For the LORD, the Most High, is awesome, a great king over all the earth.**

LEADER: Sing praises to God, sing praises; sing praises to our King, sing praises.

PEOPLE: **For God is the king of all the earth; sing praises with a psalm.**

Benediction (from Ephesians 1)

May the God of our Lord Jesus Christ give you a spirit of wisdom and revelation as you come to know him, so that with the eyes of your heart enlightened, you may know what is the hope to which he has called you, what are the riches of his glorious inheritance among the saints, and what is the immeasurable greatness of his power for us who believe.

Day of Pentecost

Elizabeth A. Pugh

Ezekiel 37:1-14: Ezekiel prophesies to the valley of dry bones.

Psalm 104:24-34, 35b: The psalmist praises the Lord for all of creation that is brought to life by God's spirit.

Acts 2:1-21: The Holy Spirit descends upon the gathered Christian believers.

John 15:26-27; 16:4b-15: Jesus promises to send the Spirit of truth, the Advocate, to dwell with believers after he has gone away.

REFLECTIONS

When you listen to the story of Acts 2 containing a cacophony of different voices, yet with a unified purpose, the preacher is given a wonderful way of thinking about the church in its particularity and uniqueness. What does this story of Pentecost tell us about the truth concerning the church? The truth about the church is that it grows and matures and survives because the winds of the spirit continue to recast the eternal message in any and every way possible. The Spirit breaks down, breaks open, and breaks out of our idolatries and our comfort levels.

Some of us struggle this day with overhead projectors, big-screen televisions, praise choruses, and any technological addition to our worship that feels irreverent and lacking in spiritual depth. Others struggle with inclusive language, feminine images of God, and new hymns. Can these different mediums and modes really share the gospel in effective and meaningful ways that will actually change lives? Only the Spirit knows!

A SERMON BRIEF
Translating the Spirit

Pentecost is about many things. It is about celebrating the birthday of the church, wearing red, and imagining the sound of rushing wind that signifies God's power and presence. But how does one describe such power and presence? Words are inadequate. Pictures are a little better. Yet ultimately, we cannot describe this reality completely.

But one clear manifestation of the spirit at the first Pentecost was the ability to speak, to communicate so that everyone, no matter who he or she was, could understand the gospel. Therefore, most important, the celebration of Pentecost is about the gift of proclamation, the spirit's amazing ability to take the gospel of Jesus and package it for all people, everywhere, *and* to have it make sense. Whether you were from Persia or Cappadocia, Asia or Egypt, or whether you were from Libya or Rome, you could understand. No common language existed and so "each one heard them speaking in his [or her] own language" (NIV). The gospel, as made known through the power of the Holy Spirit, was somehow no longer clothed in Judean garb. On Pentecost, the gospel went global; the good news was now an international commodity.

Christianity has long been on the forefront with the challenge of presenting the gospel in many different languages. The Pentecost story stands as a clear reminder of the multilingual nature of Christianity; therefore, it should come as no surprise to us that the translation of the Christian Scriptures into other languages is at the center of the Christian missionary effort. I remember a few years back hearing of a project to translate the New Testament into Klingon, the language of the mythical warlike race of the *Star Trek* television series and movies. This enterprise may offer for some "Trekkies" the first opportunity to hear the gospel in Klingon, and is an interesting strategy since Christianity is often not well accepted in the serious science fiction community.

Pentecost is a magnificent depiction of how the Holy Spirit is present, translating the gospel for any and all. Yet the deeper significance of this story of proclamation is that the gospel can be expressed in any tongue, any culture, no matter what that culture might be. Pentecost claims that the gospel story, the story of Jesus' life, death, and resurrection, can be told anywhere and at any time, effectively and meaningfully. But is this really possible? Are we really able to communicate across culture, language, and time barriers?

For instance, how should Roman Catholics celebrate the Eucharist in countries where Muslim theocracies forbid the production or importation of fermented beverages? Or how should the Methodists celebrate baptism among the Masai in Africa, where to pour water on the head of a woman is to curse her with infertility? And what do we do about the Roman Catholic discipline of clerical celibacy in a culture where not to marry and have children is seen as a curse of one's own parents? Well, maybe you and I don't have these sorts of experiences, but we still have our own cultural challenges.

For instance, Jesus used wine during the Last Supper, therefore, many Christian communities serve it as a common element in their traditional eucharistic services. So, what should be done about the reformed alcoholic, for whom even one drink is one too many? Should we rent a praise band and change all our music because we think that unchurched people will come? Do you want to get rid of our new hymnals and invest in a big-screen television monitor to display the words to praise songs? Should we alter our liturgical language to include both genders, as well as include feminine images of God? How should we do worship for those who cannot read? Should we just drop the word "church" out of our title and replace it with "worship center"? Could we allow the youngest children and babies to stay in worship because parents don't see their kids enough as it is?

As you can see, the issues involved in communicating the gospel, in every culture including our own, are very complex and need much attention. But Pentecost reminds us that the Spirit will continue to be present with us, translating the gospel in every time and place. The excitement of the coming of the Holy Spirit is that this message of Jesus, once confined to Galilean hills and small Nazareth streets, is now made available to all people, but not without our help. The messages of love, of sacrifice, and of faith are universal values, but we must continue to bring an expression to our experience that is meaningful to others.

The Holy Spirit seeks to make us more effective vessels of living the gospel, as well as telling the stories of Jesus to another who needs some help in interpretation and translation for this day. We must begin to try and speak the language of another, to use the symbols and idioms that mean something to someone else. The challenge is to free the gospel from its cage where it struggles to live, the cage of the traditional, institutional church. If people are not getting it, we need to find ways to help them get it.

The supernatural expression of the Spirit is the gift of proclamation, and its translation through us today is both a challenge and a promise. Each time I enter the pulpit, I am made even more aware that the task I have is an awesome one. Shaping the infinite in finite terms in the

125

short time I have, with the clock-watchers making sure we're out by noon, with different ages and cultures, with churched and unchurched, is the challenge. And I would say that this requires nothing less than a supernatural, Holy Spirit miracle that is no less dramatic or effective than the rush of a mighty wind or the appearance of tongues of fire.

May the good news of Jesus continue to find more marvelous vehicles for spreading through our world. May Jesus, the Word of Life, be made real in the lives of people and cut loose to do "his thing" in our day and the days to come.

SUGGESTIONS FOR WORSHIP

Call to Worship (from Acts 2)

LEADER: In the last days it will be, God declares, that I will pour out my Spirit upon all flesh,

PEOPLE: **And your sons and your daughters shall prophesy, and your young men shall see visions, and your old men shall dream dreams.**

LEADER: The sun shall be turned to darkness and the moon to blood, before the coming of the Lord's great and glorious day.

PEOPLE: **Then everyone who calls on the name of the Lord shall be saved.**

Call to Confession

God of flame and color, your life has flowed through our history, leaping from one generation to another, releasing captives, affirming the poor, welcoming outcasts. You have spoken with the accent of all people in displaying your love for all life.

Prayer of Confession

Eternal God: Your Spirit of truth has come upon us like a fresh and cleansing wind. Forgive our desire to cling to the past rather than embrace a new future, our tendency to reject your call rather than respond to new challenges, and our refusal to encounter your grace where we least expect it. Open our hearts to the gifts you offer in the accents of others and in the eternal presence of Christ our Lord. Amen.

Ordinary Time 15 or Proper 10

Brenda C. Barrows

---

2 Samuel 6:1-5, 12b-19: David and the people of Israel arrange to bring the ark of God to Jerusalem.

Psalm 24: The psalmist praises "the King of glory" and implores purity from those who seek to stand in God's holy place.

Ephesians 1:3-14: The writer to the Ephesians recounts the spiritual inheritance of those who have been redeemed through Christ.

Mark 6:14-29: The death of John the Baptist.

REFLECTIONS

The lectionary focus for 2 Samuel 6 rests on David's triumphant retrieval of the ark of God from the Philistines. An impressive army accompanies the king as he directs the ark's removal from its place of captivity. David himself leads the mighty throng in a joyous parade before the ark. As the passage progresses, so does the parade, seemingly without a hitch—unless you count the long breath the reader takes between verses 5 and 12b. I hope that all of us have church members whose curiosity leads them to their pew Bibles to find out just what those missing six-and-a-half verses have to say.

As it turns out, this lectionary gap provides an ideal vehicle for demonstrating the ways we often avoid acknowledging the dark, but integral, episodes that shape our family and faith histories. The death of David's helper, Uzzah, beside the ark, and David's fury and terror in response to God, are the "family secrets" that underlie this reading of the pericope. In the course of this sermon, I have tried not only to address the inevitable tensions of sustaining a lively relationship with God, but also to describe the inevitability of the searching, magnetic love that draws us back within God's embrace.

127

A SERMON BRIEF
Missing Pieces

Where I come from, they like to say that if you go back far enough in anyone's family, you'll find a horse thief somewhere. That's a westerner's way of putting it, but I think it tells the universal truth that most of us have pieces of our history we would rather not share. When certain parts of the family or community story are hard to explain or impossible to understand, it can be easiest just to leave out a detail or two and go on with the "good" parts.

We have a case of the "good parts" taking over in the Old Testament lesson. What the lectionary gives us is something like the story of Little Red Riding Hood—without the wolf. We set out through the woods. We come to grandmother's house. We eat what's in the basket of goodies that mother sent with us—and we all live happily ever after! And the child within us says, "Hey, wait a minute! How many pages did you skip?"

There is a shadowy, hard story in those skipped verses. We left David and his army dancing in noisy procession before the ark of God. They had the ark loaded on a cart, and (here's where we lower our voices and tell the family secret) when they got to a certain bend in the road, the man named Uzzah reached out and touched the ark. Either he thought it was going to fall, or he slipped and reached out to save himself. Whatever happened, the text says that the Lord burned with anger at Uzzah. And God struck him, and he died there beside the ark of God.

When a disaster happens in the safe and distant past, you can be sure the scholars will set out in a happy quest for the facts. Maybe Uzzah showed disrespect for the ark. Or maybe the ark was so powerful it couldn't help burning him when he got too close. In the book of Exodus, Moses gives elaborate instructions for transporting the ark. Yet Uzzah and his companions have the ark loaded onto a cart as if it were your grandmother's old piano. Something bad was bound to happen. Or was it a bigger problem, one that David brought on himself by trying to use the ark to bolster his own political power, as Walter Brueggemann suggests? It's all very interesting—at a distance.

It isn't interesting at all when tragedy strikes close to home. The child of a friend is killed in a freak accident. Others may be helped by finding out what caused the accident, but nothing we do can protect us from our grief. Or someone we love has been diagnosed with cancer. We know that she hasn't always taken good care of herself. Maybe that contributed to the illness. But what earthly use is it to mention that now, when all that really matters is for her to get well and for the nightmare to be over? We don't need or want logical explanations and assurances from our uninvolved friends that everything will work out for the best. In fact, talk like that can make us downright furious.

David was furious with God. "How can I trust you?" is the essence of what he says to God after the terrible incident with the ark. After Uzzah falls dead in the road, David refuses to bring the ark into Jerusalem. He leaves it outside the city with a family of Gittites—not even members of his own community. And there it sits for three months.

Shunning is one way of showing anger. And, whether we like it or not, anger is one way of staying related to someone. Being furious says that we care enough to be outraged. It matters! It is only when anger turns to indifference that a relationship is truly over. David may have walked away furious, but he can't find a way to be indifferent to God. And he can't help hearing about the ark of God that has been left behind.

The news about the ark seems too good to be true. The Gittite family has the ark, literally by accident, and the whole household is basking in God's blessings. You might expect David to be even angrier when he hears this, but instead, David decides to bring the ark into Jerusalem. Not only that, but he's back out there dancing in front of it again. Has he forgotten what happened?

David has *not* forgotten. This is a very different procession, and it's certainly a different David that we see. For one thing, there is no cart this time, but flesh-and-blood *people* carrying the ark like a cherished treasure. And David is out there making sacrifices before the ark, dressed as a priest. This is not a conquering king bringing home a trophy to show off to the neighbors. It's a humbled man who knows that his God is in control.

But this humbled man is not a dreary priest by any means. David is leaping before the Lord with all his might. What has gotten into him? I think it makes more sense to ask what has gotten *out* of David. This time when we see David, he has worn out and lost his anger. He has taken off his royal dignity. And he has left behind the piece of himself that had to be in charge of everything—even God. Instead of trying to move God into his life like a piece of furniture, David has given up on the notion that he could ever keep God out. And he has given in to the overwhelming pull of the grace of God that works in its own way and its own time.

God's grace doesn't work in our time or our way. That is certain. Even if we don't talk about them, most of us have some sore spots and missing pieces in our faith where we expected God to step in, and so far we have been disappointed. So far. But in spite of and from inside the whirlwind of our pain and confusion—even out of our anger and estrangement—God's grace comes to find us and calls us all, like David, back to worship. We may be weary. Our faith may have been tested by fire. But in our worship we reaffirm our faith that God is in charge. And with deepening understanding, we affirm our faith in the risen Jesus Christ, whose death was the open door to an entirely new kind of rejoicing.

SUGGESTIONS FOR WORSHIP

Call to Worship (based on Psalm 24)

ONE: The earth is the Lord's and all that is in it, the world and those who live in it.

MANY: **We belong to the Lord; we live by God's grace.**

ONE: Let us ascend the hill of the Lord and stand in God's holy place.

MANY: **Let us come with clean hands and pure hearts to seek God's face.**

ONE: Lift up your heads, O gates;

MANY: **Lift them high, O everlasting doors;**

ALL: **And the King of glory shall come in.**

Prayer of Confession and Assurance of Pardon (based on Ephesians 1)

ONE: Let us confess our sin before God and in the presence of our neighbors.

MANY: **Loving God, you have known us and chosen us from the very beginning.**
Yet we imagine ourselves in charge of your world, independent of your will. By your grace, forgive us when we try to ignore your powerful presence in our lives. Forgive us when we turn away from your saving love. Cleanse our hearts and lead us back to you. Amen.

ONE: Friends, God's grace reaches out to gather all things in him. Hear the good news: through Jesus Christ, we are forgiven. Amen.

Ordinary Time 16 or Proper 11

Ruth Patterson

---

2 Samuel 7:1-14a: Through the prophet Nathan, God promises to make David a great leader and to bless Israel with peace.

Psalm 89:20-37: God's protection and blessing of David and his descendants are confirmed.

Ephesians 2:11-22: The writer to the Ephesians reminds Christian believers of their unity in Christ Jesus and their membership in "the household of God."

Mark 6:30-34, 53-56: Jesus seeks "a deserted place" away from the crowds to rest, but his solace is interrupted by the demands of the people.

REFLECTIONS

The whole of Mark 6 is packed full of momentous events. It begins with Jesus returning to his hometown of Nazareth, teaching in front of his own folk in the local synagogue, and being rejected. There follows the sending out of the twelve apostles, their first real test where Jesus lets them go to put into practice what they have absorbed from him. Then his cousin, the one called to prepare the way for him, John the Baptist, is killed by Herod Antipas. Included also are the amazing miracles of the feeding of the five thousand and the walking on water. There is enough here of sadness and grief, of celebration and joy, of anticipation and expectancy, of amazement and wonder to fill a whole book, let alone one chapter! Surely, then, these two little clusters of verses, telling of the crowds thronging to Jesus, are incidental, fill-in sentences to link one momentous event with another. Not so. It was for these and such as these in every age that Jesus came. They were hungry—not only for bread, but for healing, for meaning, and fundamentally, even if they didn't always know it, for God.

For these Jesus spoke and was rejected at Nazareth. For such as these he sent out his disciples. Thousands were fed, and a storm was calmed from a heart moved by compassion for these sheep without a shepherd. Essentially these verses are about pilgrimage, about a pilgrim God who leaves the riches of heaven and travels home by way of the cross so that the vast crowds of every age might at least touch the fringe of his robe and be healed, restored, blessed. They are about a pilgrim people who were spurred on to be with him out of their hungering and thirsting for what he had to offer, for who he was. And if the longing behind the journey is what makes a pilgrimage sacred, then these verses are holy ground and are central to the good news.

A SERMON BRIEF

During Easter 2001, I went to Lourdes in southwest France. It is probably one of the most popular and best-known places of Catholic pilgrimage in the world. According to the statistics, five million pilgrims and visitors come to Lourdes each year, among whom are found, in vast numbers, the sick, young people, and others who come simply to pray. I was there with Faith and Light, an organization founded by Jean Vanier and Marie Hélène Matthieu that brings together people with learning disabilities, their families, and those who would like to be their friends. Its beginnings were rooted in the suffering and rejection of a husband and wife and their two profoundly physically and mentally handicapped sons who had gone to Lourdes and felt excluded and isolated. Out of that experience, in response to the cry of pain of so many parents and people with disabilities who were shut up in institutions and who were excluded from society and church, like sheep without a shepherd, Faith and Light was born. Today, thirty years later, the compassion of Jesus is tangible in these 1,400 communities from more than eighty countries. Easter 2001 was their anniversary. Sixteen hundred of us from Catholic, Protestant, and Orthodox communities came as pilgrims to celebrate and mingle with others from every race under heaven. We came not only to celebrate but to be renewed, to experience a feeling of unity while recognizing our diversity, and to be a symbol of the unique value of each individual and the place of the weakest in our societies and in our churches. We came in the brokenness that is, recognized or not, common to all humanity, that we might touch at least the fringe of his robe.

Over the few days, as we filled the streets that converged on the special places for prayer and healing and were jostled and shoved, as well as doing our fair share of pushing, all in great good humor, I could not help thinking of the crowds who thronged to Jesus long ago. They needed healing, they needed food, they needed teaching, and they needed hope.

In that multitude there would have been many of the very poor, those who were marginalized and excluded for various reasons, from society and from synagogue. There would have been those from every class who were ill, diseased, and desperate, those who would have had questions about faith, those with all sorts of political aspirations and dreams. The word would have spread like wildfire that there was someone who could help them, and from villages, cities, and farms they flocked to hear him, to be touched, to be healed, to be blessed. The need was raw. It was their need that drew them together and, in a sense, formed them into a community that waited expectantly for what was to come. Jesus, looking at them, had compassion on them because they were like sheep without a shepherd. So he taught them many things. And even those who only touched the fringe of his robe were healed.

It's like a little picture of the church—or what Jesus intended the church to be—isn't it? I feel that he wants the church—he wants us— to be a place, a community, to which people throng because they know that here they who are like sheep without a shepherd will meet with someone who will recognize their needs; who will not judge or ostracize or condemn, but who will have compassion; who will teach and feed and heal them; who will draw them to their feet so that they can stand straight in the knowledge of who they are in him.

But so often the reverse is true. We welcome those who are acceptable, who think the same way as we do, who will not embarrass us by voicing their needs too loudly. We might lose the "respectable" if we opened our doors to the marginalized, or talked too loudly about the unity in diversity that God desires for all his people. And so we miss out. We miss out on the richness of difference, on the gift that each individual brings regardless of background or ability or race or tradition. We miss out on growth and stretching. We do not hear clearly the call to pilgrimage because we have stopped seeking something more, we have stopped really believing that there is One who can teach us many things, who can heal us and feed us and bless us, so that in turn we can teach and heal and feed and bless. We certainly miss out on the vast crowds. Wherever they are, they are not thronging to be with us.

Maybe we have to come to the point, in all humility, of seeing ourselves as much part of that multitude of need as the more obvious others; that we who call ourselves people of the church have similar yearnings and questions and diseases that require the touching and the teaching of Jesus. In solidarity with all our sisters and brothers, we are a community of the broken. It is when we bring our brokenness together, across all the walls that people would seek to erect between us and which Jesus again and again persists in knocking down, that he builds his temple, his true church. In our vulnerability we begin to see others in the crowd as our sisters and brothers. We recognize the voice of the Shepherd whose heart toward his "sheep" is always one of compassion. In faith we reach out to touch the fringe of his robe and to know ourselves, restored, members of his family, carefully joined together, in the process of becoming a holy temple for him, and in ourselves, a place of pilgrimage where others can see and touch him.

SUGGESTIONS FOR WORSHIP

Litany of Unity (adapted from Ephesians 2)

LEADER: Remember that we were at one time without Christ, strangers to the covenants of promise, having no hope and without God in the world.

PEOPLE: **But now in Christ Jesus, we who once were far off have been brought near by the blood of Christ.**

LEADER: For he is our peace; in his flesh he has made us all into one and has broken down the dividing walls between us.

PEOPLE: **So now we are no longer strangers and aliens, but we are citizens with the saints and members of the household of God.**

LEADER: We are built upon the foundation of the apostles and prophets, with Christ Jesus himself as the cornerstone.

PEOPLE: **In him the whole structure is joined together and grows into a holy temple in the Lord, in whom we are built together spiritually into a dwelling place for God.**

Ordinary Time 30 or Proper 25

Tracy Hartman

Job 42:1-6, 10-17: Job acknowledges the wise and wonderful ways of God, and his fortunes are restored twofold.

Psalm 34:1-8 (19-22): The psalmist gives personal testimony to God's faithfulness in delivering the righteous.

Hebrews 7:23-28: The everlasting priesthood of Christ and his ability to save those who approach God through him are confirmed.

Mark 10:46-52: Jesus heals blind Bartimaeus as he and the disciples travel through Jericho.

REFLECTIONS

The Gospel text is about insiders and outsiders. Jesus uses the physical healing of blind Bartimaeus, an outsider, to illustrate the spiritual blindness of the disciples, who considered themselves insiders.[1] Bartimaeus is not willing to remain an outsider; he is not willing to function within the boundaries of his station. Despite admonishment from the crowd, Bartimaeus persists in calling out to Jesus. He knows what he wants, and he is not afraid to ask for it. Then, after his healing, and without specific invitation, he follows Jesus "on the way."[2]

After Bartimaeus gains the attention of Jesus, Jesus asks him, "What do you want me to do for you?" Earlier, Jesus had asked this question of James and John. Their request was for special treatment in heaven, and Jesus was not happy with them. Unlike the disciples, Bartimaeus's request is sincere and straightforward. Jesus does not hesitate to grant his petition.

After his healing, Jesus tells Bartimaeus to go. Instead, Bartimaeus leaves his cloak, his only worldly possession, and follows after Jesus. This action is in stark contrast to the rich young ruler who could not leave his treasures to follow. For his actions throughout the story, Bartimaeus is seen as a model of true faith.

Lamar Williamson points out that this text functions as both a miracle story and a call story. It is a miracle story because Bartimaeus's sight is miraculously restored. However, the actual healing is downplayed in the text. It is considered a call story because, similar to other stories in Mark, it tells how a specific person whose name is given (which is uncharacteristic of miracle stories) becomes a follower of Christ. Willliamson also connects this passage to Jeremiah 31:7-9, an oracle of salvation and restoration. In that text, the Lord promises to gather God's people from the farthest parts of the earth, "among them the blind and the lame."[3]

A SERMON BRIEF

Think with me for a moment about someone you have misjudged. Perhaps someone you didn't care for at first turned out to be a trusted friend. Or someone at work who didn't appear competent turned out to be your best employee. Many now famous people were once misjudged. Walt Disney seemed like an unlikely candidate to produce animated films—a newspaper editor once fired him because he "lacked imagination and had no good ideas." Madeleine L'Engle did not seem destined to become a renowned author—her Newbery Medal–winning book, *A Wrinkle in Time*, was rejected by countless publishers who didn't want to take a chance on it. Michael Jordan appeared to be an unlikely candidate for professional basketball—he was cut from his high school basketball team. And no one would have expected Oprah Winfrey to become one of the wealthiest and most influential women in America. She was born to unmarried parents in rural Mississippi, shuffled between family members as a child, and even abused by another relative. Nor did anyone expect Albert Einstein to be a genius—he didn't speak a word until he was four. One of Thomas Edison's teachers certainly did not think he would be a great inventor. She told him he was too stupid to learn anything. He was counseled to go into a field where he might succeed by virtue of his pleasant personality.

Upon an initial reading of our Gospel text, no one would expect that Bartimaeus would end up being a model of faith. After all, he is a beggar—and a blind, annoying one at that. Don't you see him, sitting there on the side of the road? His robe is tattered and torn, and his cloak—his only possession—is spread out beneath him. His walking stick lies across his lap. Day after day he is there, begging, "Alms for the poor, alms for the poor." Only wait, today is different. A crowd is coming down the road, and there is a sense of urgency in Bartimaeus's voice. He must want to maximize the opportunity to fill his cup. But no, he is calling out something different today. What is that he is saying? Then you catch the new words: "Jesus, Son of David, have mercy on me! Jesus, Son of David, have mercy on me!" Bartimaeus is pleading for more than coins today, and the people on the side of the road try to silence him. You can hear them now. "Be quiet Bartimaeus. Leave Jesus alone. You're just an old, blind beggar. What makes you think Jesus would have time for you? Be quiet!"

But Bartimaeus doesn't seem to know his place, for he persists even more urgently, "Jesus, Son of David, have mercy on me! Jesus, Son of David, have mercy on me!" And then it happens. The crowd is stunned. Jesus stops and turns toward Bartimaeus. "Call him here," the Master says. The tone of the crowd changes instantly as they call to Bartimaeus. "Get up!" they cry. "Jesus is calling for you." Immediately Bartimaeus springs up. His walking stick is tapping in front of him as he makes his way to Jesus. Then Jesus looks at Bartimaeus, looks him right in the eye, and asks, "What do you want me to do for you?"

Those who followed Jesus had heard him ask James and John the same question earlier. And, you might recall, Jesus was none too happy with *their* answer. They asked the Master for a place of honor beside him in heaven. After all, they were insiders, faithful disciples. They believed it was well within their right to ask. But Jesus obviously didn't agree, and he explained that those who wanted to be first would be last, and those who were last would be first.

Now here is Bartimaeus, certainly one of the last, begging Jesus for mercy. How will he answer the Master's question? The spectators hold their breath, waiting to see what Bartimaeus will say. His request turns out to be simple, and humble. "My teacher," he asks, "let me see again."

All eyes turn to Jesus. How will he respond? Will he lay hands on Bartimaeus, or make a paste from the dirt and his spittle as he had done before? But this time Jesus does nothing. He merely speaks these words, "Go; your faith has made you well." Instantly, Bartimaeus regains his sight. But he doesn't go anywhere. In fact, he follows Jesus on the way. He never did listen well, that Bartimaeus. Unlike the rich young ruler who refused to leave his many possessions to follow Jesus, Bartimaeus left his own cloak right there on the side of the road and followed after Christ.

The disciples probably were not happy to have Bartimaeus with them. After all, he wasn't one of them. He was an outsider, not an insider. He hadn't been with Jesus for years. What could he possibly know? Sure, he was exuberant. After all, Jesus had just healed him. But he hadn't been there for the long haul. But you know, sometimes those disciples just didn't get it. And of all people, they should have gotten it. They had been with Jesus for three years; they had been there for the long haul. But sometimes they just didn't understand. I guess you could say they were spiritually blind. They didn't understand that Jesus came to heal them of their spiritual blindness just like he healed Bartimaeus of his physical blindness. They didn't understand that Jesus came to make outsiders insiders and the last the first. They didn't understand that Bartimaeus, in his sincerity and persistence, could be a model for all of us. They just didn't get it. After all, Bartimaeus seemed like such an unlikely candidate.

SUGGESTIONS FOR WORSHIP

Call to Worship (adapted from Psalm 34)

LEADER:	Let us bless the LORD at all times;
PEOPLE:	**God's praise shall continually be in our mouths.**
LEADER:	My soul makes its boast in the LORD;
PEOPLE:	**Let the humble hear and be glad.**
LEADER:	O magnify the LORD with me,
PEOPLE:	**And let us exalt God's name together.**

Unison Prayer
(suggested for use after the sermon)

Eternal God: You sent your Son to comfort the afflicted and afflict the comfortable. Make us gracious receivers of your transforming love; through Christ our example and Lord, Amen.

---

1. Lamar Williamson, "Mark" in *Interpretation Commentary* (Atlanta: John Knox Press, 1983), 197.
2. Ibid., 198.
3. Ibid.

All Saints Day

Florence E. Canada

Isaiah 25:6-9: The Lord of hosts, for whom the people have waited, will wipe away all tears and disgrace from the people and grant them salvation.

Psalm 24: Only those with clean hands and pure hearts can ascend the hill of the Lord, the dwelling place of the King of glory.

Revelation 21:1-6a: The vision of the new heaven and the new earth.

John 11:32-44: Jesus raises Lazarus from death to life.

REFLECTIONS

I am thankful that God does not run away from death. As a matter of fact, God runs toward it with a call from death to life. We could view the entire Bible as a call from death to life. In opening chapters, God creates the heavens and the earth out of nothing, and in the closing chapters, God promises a world that is made new—a world that is free from sin, sorrow, sickness, and even death. The coming of Jesus Christ into the world represents the personification of God's call out of death and into life. It is a call that has eternal ramifications in the call from death to sin to eternal life in Jesus. However, it is also a call that has ramifications for our daily lives. Jesus is not just calling us to life in eternity. He is calling us from death to life right now.

A SERMON BRIEF

The Call from Death to Life

In the natural order of things, we are taught that people live and then die. However, in the resurrection of Lazarus, we see a different order of things. We see that when Jesus is present, the call that is extended is a call from death to life. In other words, in the presence of the divine, that which is dead can live again.

Martha and Mary were distraught over the death of their brother. The grief they felt held an added dimension of sorrow and disbelief, even a tinge of anger. They had sent word to Jesus of Lazarus's condition, believing that if Jesus could get there in time, he would be able to heal their brother. Jesus would be able to raise him up from his bed of affliction. They sent the message, and they waited—and waited. Days passed, and Lazarus grew sicker. Still Jesus did not come. Lazarus continued to grow sicker and weaker; still Jesus did not come. Then, Lazarus died.

Finally, after Lazarus was already dead, Jesus arrived. We can feel the anguish in Mary's voice as she meets Jesus and falls at his feet crying, "Lord, if you had been here, my brother would not have died." At this particular moment, when confronted with death, it was impossible for Mary to see beyond her anguish and loss.

It was evident to everyone present how much Jesus had loved Lazarus. Jesus was so moved that he himself wept. He wept in his own grief, and he wept at the sight of the grief, hopelessness, and despair around him. But Jesus' concern did not end with weeping. He instructed some of the men in the crowd to roll the stone away from the door of Lazarus's tomb. The men were hesitant—Lazarus had been dead for four days. What good would it do? Besides, the stench of decomposing flesh was already powerful. What was the use of rolling away the stone? What could Jesus possibly do now? Lazarus was already long dead.

But Jesus saw beyond the hopelessness of the moment to the possibilities open to those who trust in God. "Did I not tell you that if you believed, you would see the glory of God?" he said to Martha. Those gathered around the tomb are about to experience the power of God in a way that will forever alter their view of reality and shatter their understanding of life and death.

The stone is rolled away, and Jesus, looking toward heaven, thanks God for answering his prayer in the presence of the skeptical crowd. "Lazarus, come out!" he cries with a loud voice. And to the surprise of everyone in the crowd, Lazarus walks out of the tomb still wrapped in the clothes of burial. Jesus commands them to remove the burial clothes, for Lazarus, who was dead, is now alive.

Friends, there is good news in the response of our Savior to death. Jesus wept. In that simple verse (11:35), we can feel the love and compassion of our Savior. He came not that we should die, but that we should live. But notice: Jesus' response did not *end* with tears—he moved to action. He called Lazarus forth from death to life. And the *really* good news is that Jesus is still doing the same today. He takes that which is dead and gives it new life. After all, if Jesus could resurrect Lazarus, doesn't that mean that he can resurrect the dead things in *our* lives? Doesn't that mean he will not be put off by the stench and decay of death, no matter where he encounters it? Isn't he willing to get close enough to call us forth from death to life, too? The answer is a resounding Yes! Jesus takes the things that others have given up on—broken lives, damaged relationships, devastated communities—and he calls them forth from death to life.

It is this knowledge that Jesus calls dead things to life that motivates me to pastor a church in the inner city. The community around the church shows signs of urban blight—poverty, crime, neglect, hopelessness, and despair. However, as we live the love of Jesus through worship, praise, and ministry, slowly that which has been dead is experiencing new life. Men, women, and children are being called forth from the death of sin to life. They are being called forth from the death of despair and poverty to life filled with hope and prosperity. I believe, before it is all over, that the entire community will once again bustle with the sounds of life!

Brothers and sisters, God is calling now. God is calling the dead parts of our being. God is calling the dead communities in our city. God is calling to churches that have grown dead and cold. All around us, God is calling, calling all of creation back from death to life.

I noticed that Jesus told the people who gathered at Lazarus's tomb that if they only believed, they would experience the glory of God. Indeed, the first step in experiencing the new life to which Jesus calls is to believe. We must believe that he has the power to resurrect what is dead, even what is dead in our own lives. You see, believing in resurrection power is the key to experiencing the glory of resurrection.

Several years ago, God called me to move into a neighborhood that was filled with the stench of death. Half of my street was boarded up. The house next to mine was a frequent hangout for prostitutes and addicts. But God spoke and said, "Over the next five years, I am going to transform this neighborhood. I am calling it back from death to life." God placed me there to be a witness to the power of resurrection. Eventually, God sent others who also believed. Now, several years later, old houses have been torn down and new houses have been built. Children play outside, and neighbors greet each other as they come and go.

Friends, God is calling. God is calling us from death to life. Let us believe we will see God's glory and go forth in faith.

SUGGESTIONS FOR WORSHP

Call to Worship
(adapted from Psalm 24:7-10)

LEADER: Lift up your heads, O you gates; be lifted up, you ancient doors, that the King of glory may come in.
PEOPLE: **Who is this King of glory?**
ALL: **The LORD strong and mighty, the LORD mighty in battle.**
LEADER: Lift up your heads, O you gates; lift them up, you ancient doors, that the King of glory may come in.
PEOPLE: **Who is he, this King of glory?**
ALL: **The LORD Almighty—he is the King of glory.**

Prayer
(inspired by Isaiah 25:6-9 and
Revelation 21:1-65*a*)

Gracious and Loving God, we look forward to the day when you will wipe away the tears from every face. We look forward to the day when there will be no more sorrow and no more pain. We look forward to the day when all the earth shall dwell in the bounty of your peace. We look forward to that day, Lord, when there will be no more death. We look forward to that day when all of your Creation will bask in the glory of your presence. Until then, Lord, please give us the strength and the courage to face death wherever we encounter it and boldly proclaim your call from death to life. In the name of Jesus we pray. Amen.

Benediction

As you go, brothers and sisters, go in the name of the King of Glory. He is the One who gives us life and sustains us. May you rest in his peace until we meet again.

Christ the King (or Reign of Christ) Sunday

Loretta Reynolds

---

2 Samuel 23:1-7: The last words of David.

Psalm 132:1-12 (13-18): A psalm singing the praises of David.

Revelation 1:4b-8: John greets the seven churches in Asia in the name of Jesus, the "Alpha and the Omega."

John 18:33-37: Jesus appears before Pilate to claim his kingship.

REFLECTIONS

As he stands before Pilate in the Gospel text, Jesus redefines kingship. Jesus rejects the earthly concept of king, which the crowds tried to force onto him. More often than we care to admit, we are with the crowd, waving palm branches and seeking a king with a golden crown and purple robes. Like them, we will discover that a king who calls us to follow in the way of service, obedience, and even death is a difficult king to follow. This king is so far from our expectations and desires that we often are unable to recognize him as a king. Jesus insisted that he was the revealer of God and that his purpose was not to call attention to himself, but to reveal God and God's kingdom. Jesus warned his followers that the road to his kingdom would be difficult and narrow.

A SERMON BRIEF

What Kind of King Is This?

Pilate struggled to understand whether or not Jesus was a king. He was not greatly invested in this question, but he was holding a human

143

life in his hands. We should have some sympathy with Pilate's confusion. Many people said Jesus was king of the Jews, yet there was a crowd outside Pilate's door demanding that this man be killed. Even when asked, Jesus explained that his kingdom was not of this world—it was a different kind of kingdom altogether. Pilate inquires, "So, are you a king?" Jesus' answer is both yes and no—yes to being a king, but no to the traditional concept of king. Jesus says he comes to bear witness to the truth. This doesn't sound like any kind of king Pilate knows. So Pilate is left even more confused—"What is truth?" And with the question that has echoed through history, Pilate walks out and leaves a monumental decision to the angry cries of a mob.

Pilate's confusion was really no different from others. For hundreds of years people had watched and hoped for the Messiah. Yet there were so many different expectations of the kind of king and kingdom that would come. How would they know when it arrived? How would they know which expectation would be correct?

Many believed the kingdom of God would be a re-creation of the reign of King David. The Messiah would be a great ruler with a magnificent kingdom. His would be a political kingdom that would provide safety and power for the children of Israel. This Messiah would be a military, political, and social leader. Other expectations included a figure coming down from heaven; a teacher of righteousness; a prophet like Elijah; and a doer of signs and miracles.

Sometimes we can have so many expectations that when the real thing comes we miss it altogether. The expectations of the crowds and even of the disciples were so different from who Jesus really was that many missed him. They couldn't get past their expectations of what the king should be, of what they wanted him to be. After all, what kind of king is born in a stable? What kind of king wanders around the countryside with common folk rather than amassing an army? What kind of king teaches women, eats with traitors, and holds little children in his lap? What kind of king washes his followers' feet? How could anyone be expected to believe that this man Jesus was a king?

Many who followed Jesus sought power and pomp and everything that is associated with royalty. Jesus was, at best, a point of conflict and confusion. At worst, he was a disappointment and a threat. Who wants a king who is vulnerable? Who wants a king who, instead of fighting, says you should turn the other cheek? Who wants a king who talks more about loving your enemies than about conquering them?

Is it any wonder they were confused? The people of Jesus' day are not alone. The church has struggled ever since to reconcile human expectations of kingship with the reality of who Jesus was. It would be much easier to follow a regal, powerful king than a peasant who talks about feeding the poor. As we celebrate Christ the King Sunday we want this to be a day of blasting trumpets and royal robes. We want a crown and a throne and a lot of happy smiling faces. We are still looking for the king who will shatter political realms and provide us with comfort, success, and power over our enemies. Are we not a lot like our first-century counterparts? How often do we use religion to gain political and social power? We want to believe that following Jesus will provide safety, security, and success. We want to follow a Jesus who will take away all of our problems and protect us from all harm. We want a king who is comfortable in multimillion-dollar church complexes. Recent books and training manuals even compare Jesus to the modern-day concept of king—the CEO. I wonder what Jesus would have thought about that.

We really are not much different from Jesus' first disciples, are we? They wanted to sit with Jesus in his mighty, glorious kingdom. Even though Jesus kept telling them his kingdom was nothing like that, they never quite got it—and maybe, neither do we. Jesus' reign pointed toward the truth found in God—the God of self-giving love and open-ended grace to all who will hear the truth and respond. Jesus made it clear that he was not an earthly king and that the kingdom of God was not built on physical power and force, but on love, faithfulness, and grace.

Maybe we don't get it because we don't want to get it. Crowns and thrones and power are a lot more fun and a lot less demanding than a king who says to do good to those who abuse you. Jesus said his purpose was to bear witness to the truth. Yet, speaking the truth of God brought Jesus into direct conflict with humanly generated institutions and governments. If we follow this king, should we not expect the same?

So, what kind of king is this? What kind of king rides on a donkey? What kind of king weeps over the plight of his people? What kind of king hangs on a cross?

What kind of king is this? Jesus is the kind of king who bears witness to God's love and grace. He is the kind of king who preaches the gospel to the poor, and proclaims release to the captives. This king proclaims recovery of sight to the blind, and sets free those who are downtrodden (Luke 4:18).

Today, as we leave this place, which king will we follow? Will we follow the king of our own created, self-serving expectations, or the king who Jesus proclaimed himself to be? I wonder.

SUGGESTIONS FOR WORSHIP

Call to Worship

ONE: O God, we gather here to worship you.
ALL: **We honor you as our King. We desire to follow you.**
ONE: Fill us with your gentle power and quiet strength.
ALL: **Guide us as we seek to live in your way.**

Prayer of Confession

ALL: **Hosanna! Blessed is he who comes in the name of the Lord, even the King of Israel!**
ONE: Why is this king riding a donkey?
ALL: **Hosanna! Blessed is he who is strong and mighty, even the King of Israel!**
ONE: Why is this king being beaten?
ALL: **Hosanna! Blessed is he who conquers in battle, even the King of Israel!**
ONE: Where is his army? Why is this king alone?
ALL: **Hosanna! Blessed is he who comes in the name of the Lord, even the King of Israel!**
ONE: Why is this king hanging on a cross?
ALL: **O God, forgive us when we get so caught up in our own expectations of who we want your Son to be that we miss the truth of who you are.**

Assurance of Pardon

Jesus said, take up your cross and follow me. I will forgive your sins and give you rest. In the name of God the Almighty, we are forgiven.

Benediction

As you go through the moments of your life, may God who is the Alpha and the Omega, who is and who was and who is to come, be with you now and forevermore. Amen.

Contributors

Brenda C. Barrows serves as Registrar for Union Theological Seminary and the Presbyterian School of Christian Education as well as a regular guest preacher at area churches. At her 1998 graduation from Union-PSCE, Brenda received the E. T. George Prize for Excellence in Homiletics, Worship, and Public Speaking as well as the Patrick D. Miller Award for Excellence in the Study of Scripture. She is a published poet and enjoys the arts in all manifestations.

Donna Hopkins Britt is the pastor of Calvary Baptist Church in Roanoke, Virginia. In 1994, Donna received the Chevis and Helen Horne Preaching Award at Baptist Theological Seminary in Richmond, Virginia. Several of her writings have appeared in *Homily Service*, a publication of the Liturgical Conference. Donna shares life in Roanoke with her husband, "the very supportive Brian Britt."

Florence E. Canada is the founding pastor of Living Water Christian Fellowship and president of New Genesis, Inc., a Christian ministry focused on Christian education and economic empowerment, as well as a Ph.D. student in the area of Christian education. She has served as an Adjunct Instructor in Christian Education at Virginia Union University School of Theology in Richmond. One of Florence's primary interests is helping the church develop and implement models designed to meet the needs of persons living in the inner city. She believes the church should be an agent of understanding, hope, and transformation. Her hobbies include reading a good book and visiting with family and friends.

Felecia T. Douglass is a minister in the Presbyterian Church (USA). A native of Missouri, she has served churches in Missouri, North Carolina, and Virginia. Upon graduation from seminary, she received an award for excellence in the study and practice of preaching. She, her husband, and their two sons live in Richmond, Virginia, where she is working on a Ph.D. in Christian Education at Union-PSCE and serving as a supply preacher for churches in the community.

Elizabeth Bridges Ford serves as Associate Pastor of Grace Presbyterian Church, Jenkintown, Pennsylvania. Three years traveling with the Smithsonian Institution and a year studying theology in Montpelier, France, enabled Beth to indulge her passion for the arts, travel, and fine food. Now she enjoys writing, spending time with friends, and visiting offbeat museums.

Tracy Hartman serves on the adjunct faculty of the Baptist Theological Seminary at Richmond in the areas of Christian Ministry and Homiletics. She is also Associate Director of the seminary's Chevis Horne Center for Preaching and Worship and interim pastor of Menokin Baptist Church in Warsaw, Virginia. A recent recipient of a Ph.D. in Practical Theology from Union-PSCE, Tracy lives in Richmond with her husband and two children.

Vicki G. Lumpkin is the pastor of CityChurch: A Baptist Community of Grace, a new church meeting in the Uptown area of Dallas, Texas. She is a graduate of the Baptist Theological Seminary at Richmond and Union-PSCE. In her spare time, she enjoys visiting and photographing Christian worship space. She is married to the Reverend Charles D. Lumpkin.

Marjorie A. Menaul is Rector of St. Paul's Episcopal Church in Bloomsburg, Pennsylvania. Marjorie enjoys an eclectic mix of activities and companions, including gardening, drinking coffee, reading science fiction, and spending time with one little beagle and two very large cats.

Katherine Thomas Paisley is a Ph.D. candidate at Vanderbilt University, Nashville, Tennessee. Kathy is an ordained United Methodist minister who served congregations in Middle Tennessee before returning to full-time graduate study. In her previous (pre-seminary) life, she was a Director of Music, Director of Christian Education, and Youth Director. She is blessed in living with her true mate of more than twenty-two years and three wonderful children—two in college and one toddler—who bless her with many insights and stories. She is in the dissertation stage of her Ph.D. in Homiletics and Church History under the wise supervision of David Buttrick, who is not to be held responsible for any bad moves in the sermon!

Ruth Patterson is a Presbyterian minister in Northern Ireland who currently serves as Director of Restoration Ministries, an interdenominational organization seeking to promote peace and reconciliation. Her university experience includes Queen's University, Belfast; University of Toronto, Canada; and Edinburgh University, Scotland, where she did her theological training. While at Edinburgh, she applied to be a candidate for ministry of the Presbyterian Church in Ireland, and in 1976 became the first woman to be ordained in Ireland. Her first book, *A Farther Shore*, was published in March 2000 and recounts her personal journey in prose and verse. Last year Ruth was named "University of Edinburgh/Royal Bank of Scotland Alumnus of the Year 2000." In May 2001, Ruth received an honorary Doctorate from the Presbyterian Theological Faculty of Ireland.

Elizabeth A. Pugh is Pastor of Grace Baptist Church in Richmond, Virginia. She also serves on the adjunctive faculty of the Baptist Theological Seminary at Richmond as Professor of Christian Ministry and on several denominational and institutional boards. In 2000, she was awarded an Honorary Doctor of Divinity degree by the University of Richmond, her alma mater. In between church and community responsibilities, Betty enjoys volleyball, softball, step and floor aerobics, strength training, and choral and solo vocal work.

Loretta Reynolds is Campus Chaplain at Berea College in Berea, Kentucky. Loretta holds a Doctor of Theology in Homiletics and Pastoral Care from Melbourne College of Divinity, Melbourne, Australia. In addition to her chaplain's responsibilities, she enjoys serving as a supervisor for the continuing education course "Homiletic Supervision" at Louisville Presbyterian Theological Seminary. She has worked in Botswana, British Virgin Islands, Switzerland, and Australia. She and her husband are the proud owners of a young ninety-five-pound Bernese (Swiss) Mountain Dog.

Gail Anderson Ricciuti is Associate Professor of Homiletics at Colgate Rochester Crozer Divinity School in Rochester, New York. Ordained in the Presbyterian Church (USA), she brings to her teaching some twenty-five years' pastoral experience in churches in eastern Ohio and western New York, most recently as copastor of the Downtown United Presbyterian Church in Rochester. She has served her denomination as Vice Moderator of the General Assembly (1977) and Moderator of her presbytery. Gail is coauthor of the two-volume *Birthings and Blessings: Liberating Worship Services for the Inclusive Church*.

Elaine G. Siemsen is Adjunct Professor of Preaching at Luther Seminary, St. Paul, Minnesota. An ordained minister in the Evangelical Lutheran Church of America, she serves churches in rural southeastern Minnesota as an interim pastor. Elaine finds refreshment in gardening, playing with her dog Kinzie, and spending time with her family. Her preaching interests include preaching and Christology, and preaching and contemporary Christian music.

Beverly A. Zink-Sawyer is Associate Professor of Preaching and Worship at Union Theological Seminary and Presbyterian School of Christian Education in Richmond, Virginia. A minister in the Presbyterian Church (USA), she served churches in Pennsylvania and Tennessee for fifteen years. Beverly was a Lilly Faculty Fellow of the Association of Theological Schools for the year 2000–2001 and is working on a book on three of the first clergywomen in America. She shares life in Richmond with her wonderful husband Steve and their feline "child" Charis.

Index

Subject Index

151

Scripture Index